inside
SPEED
machines

Discovery
expl⊙re
YOUR WORLD™

inside SPEED machines

By Steve Parker
Illustrated by Alex Pang

Miles Kelly

First published in 2010 by Miles Kelly Publishing Ltd
Harding's Barn, Bardfield End Green, Thaxted, Essex, CM6 3PX, UK

This edition printed in 2012

10 9 8 7 6 5 4 3 2 1

Publishing Director: *Belinda Gallagher*
Creative Director: *Jo Cowan*
Creative Concept: *Simon Lee*
Volume Design: *Rocket Design*
Cover Designer: *Simon Lee*
Indexer: *Gill Lee*
Production Manager: *Elizabeth Collins*
Reprographics: *Stephan Davis, Thom Allaway*
Consultants: *John and Sue Becklake*
Edition Editor: *Amanda Askew*

ISBN 978-1-84810-833-2

Printed in China

British Library Cataloguing-in-Publication Data
A catalogue record for this book is available from the British Library

Every effort has been made to acknowledge the source and copyright
holder of each picture. Miles Kelly Publishing apologises for any
unintentional errors or omissions.

MADE WITH PAPER FROM
A SUSTAINABLE FOREST

ACKNOWLEDGEMENTS

All panel artworks by Rocket Design
The publishers would like to thank the following
sources for the use of their photographs:
Alamy: 32 Ruby
Corbis: 6(t) Hulton-Deutsch Collection;
14 Bettmann; 27 Hulton-Deutsch Collection;
36 Bettmann
Getty Images: 6(b) AFP, (c) Curventa; 13 Mike Hewitt/
Staff; 35 Time & Life Pictures
Rex Features: 7(b) VIZO; 9 Mission; 22 Kevin Holt/
Daily Mail; 25 Newspix
Science Photo Library: 30 NASA
Topfoto.co.uk: 17 Topham Picturepoint
Shutterstock: COVER Ahmad Faizal Yahya, Walter G
Arce; 11 Walter G Arce; 18; 20 Thomas Nord; 28 Gail
Johnson
All other photographs are from Miles Kelly Archives

WWW.FACTSFORPROJECTS.COM

Each top right-hand page directs
you to the Internet to help you
find out more. You can log on
to **www.factsforprojects.com**
to find free pictures, additional
information, videos, fun activities
and further web links. These
are for your own personal use
and should not be copied or
distributed for any commercial
or profit-related purpose.

If you do decide to use the
Internet with your book, here's a
list of what you'll need:
• A PC with Microsoft® Windows®
 XP or later versions, or a
 Macintosh with OS X or later,
 and 512Mb RAM

• A browser such as Microsoft®
 Internet Explorer 9, Firefox 4.X
 or Safari 5.X
• Connection to the Internet.
 Broadband connection
 recommended.
• An account with an Internet
 Service Provider (ISP)
• A sound card for listening to
 sound files

Links won't work?
www.factsforprojects.com is
regularly checked to make sure
the links provide you with lots
of information. Sometimes you
may receive a message saying
that a site is unavailable. If this
happens, just try again later.

Stay safe!
When using the Internet, make
sure you follow these guidelines:
• Ask a parent's or a guardian's
 permission before you log on.
• Never give out your personal
 details, such as your name,
 address or email.
• If a site asks you to log in or
 register by typing your name
 or email address, speak to your
 parent or guardian first.
• If you do receive an email from
 someone you don't know, tell
 an adult and do not reply to the
 message.
• Never arrange to meet anyone
 you have talked to on the
 Internet.

www.mileskelly.net
info@mileskelly.net

CONTENTS

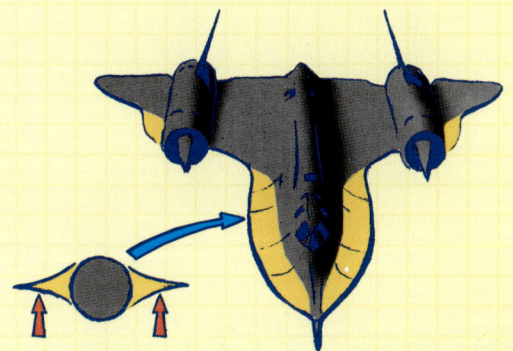

INTRODUCTION

People have always wanted to travel faster, higher and further. In Greece more than 2500 years ago, ancient Olympians celebrated human achievements by staging athletic events. As new ways of travelling were invented, people competed using these too. Horses and chariots, then sailboats, trains, bicycles, cars, speedboats, planes and rockets, created many new kinds of speed records. To be the fastest resulted in fame, status, respect, your name in history – and maybe a big money prize.

In the 1920s, cars such as this *Bentley* reached then-amazing speeds of 200 km/h.

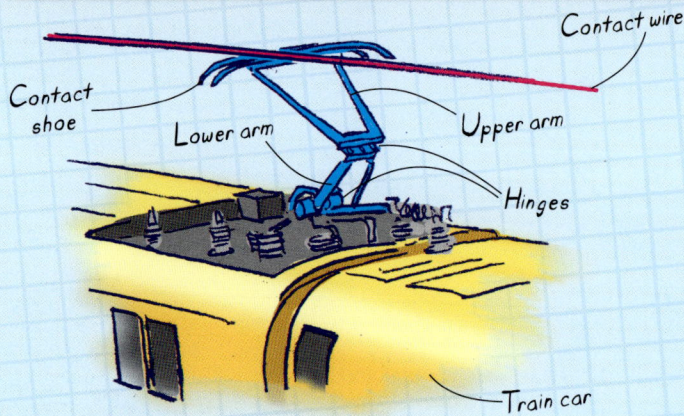

Contact wire

Contact shoe

Lower arm

Upper arm

Hinges

Train car

Electric trains are fast, but they need specialized equipment to pick up the current.

PICKING UP SPEED

As each new wave of technology and engineering came along, people applied it to speed machines. For example, steam trains battled each other for the rail record during the first half of the last century. Then along came electric trains, which travelled almost twice as fast as their steam cousins. Recently, maglev trains have taken the rail record, nudging 600 kilometres per hour.

JUST RIGHT

Attempts at speed records are a huge gamble. For example, it takes months to get a boat ready for a record-breaking venture. Then, on the day, the wind may die away for a sailboat, or it could be too strong for a powerboat. Some jet-powered water speed records have failed because ducks and geese got in the way, bobbing on the surface or almost flying into the jet engine.

Sail records continue to be set. In 2009, the trimaran Hydroptere reached a speed of 95 km/h.

The vehicles in this book are Internet linked.
Visit www.factsforprojects.com to find out more.

THE SPEED TEAM

Extreme speed machines need lots of dedicated back-up. Teams of engineers, mechanics and other helpers push technology to the limits, with constant delicate adjustments, plenty of fuel and spare parts, and complicated equipment to make sure everything runs smoothly. Everyone must pay huge attention to each tiny detail. A few specks of dirt in the fuel could make the engine cut out at a critical moment and cause disaster.

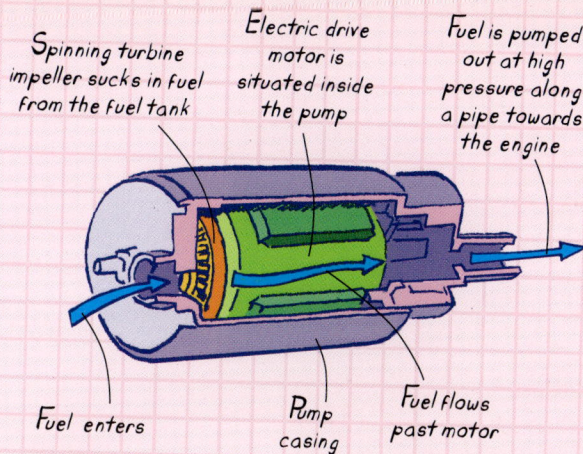

Spinning turbine impeller sucks in fuel from the fuel tank

Electric drive motor is situated inside the pump

Fuel is pumped out at high pressure along a pipe towards the engine

Fuel enters

Pump casing

Fuel flows past motor

More power requires more fuel, so fuel pump design continually improves.

THE NEED FOR SPEED

Speed aces are brave. Drivers, riders and pilots put their lives on the line. Some records are tremendously difficult to break – the water speed record was set more than 30 years and shows little sign of being broken. In the meantime, progress brings fresh challenges for new types of vehicles and craft. Today, many of these are kinder to the environment, using solar power or fuel cells. Speed machines are becoming clean machines.

Russia's Tu-144 resembled Concorde. But the era of supersonic airliners is over.

Bloodhound SSC aims to break the magic 1500 km/h land speed record.

The future may see speed records for hover-cars, personal jet-packs, human-powered aircraft and even a return trip into orbit – a race into space.

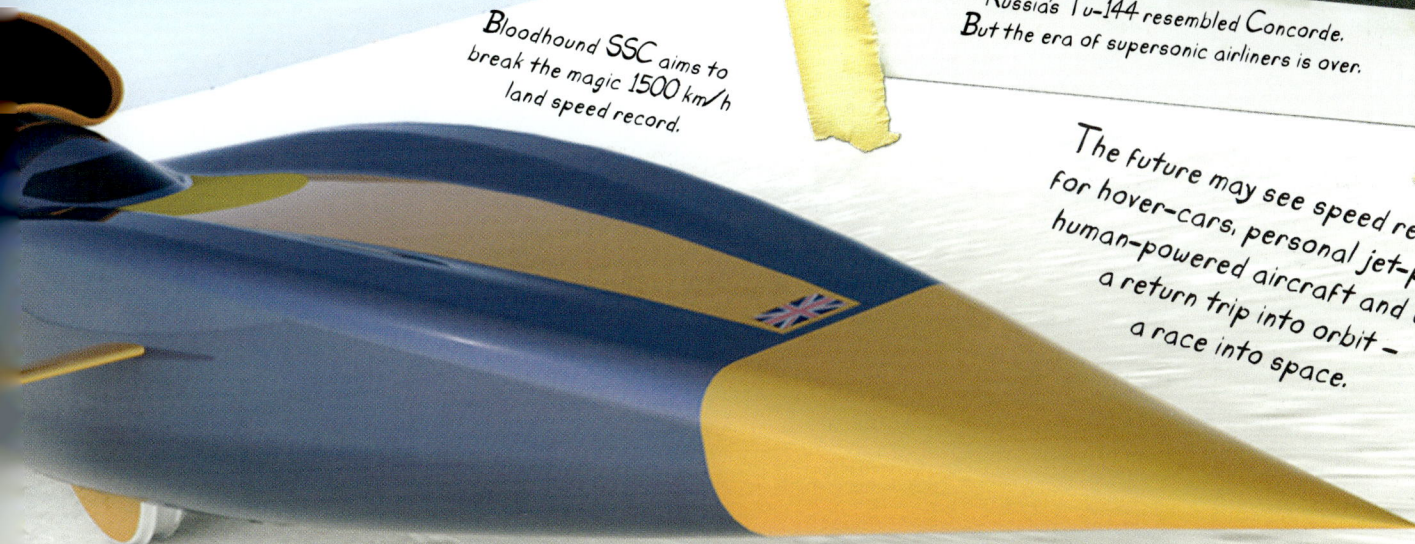

YAMAHA R1 SUPERBIKE

Ever since people started to add engines to their two-wheeled cycles, they have raced against each other and the clock. Travelling at speed on two wheels is dangerous because the rider must stay perfectly balanced and in firm contact with the ground. A sideways gust of wind, a pebble on the track or dabbing the brake at the wrong time could spell disaster – a rider has no bodywork protection on a motorcycle.

Eureka!

The biggest championship in motorcycle racing is MotoGP, which started in 1949. It grew out of unofficial races on ordinary roads in the 1930s. These were exceptionally dangerous because normal traffic was often using the roads at the same time.

Whatever next?

Small hovercraft-type motorbikes and jet-propelled bikes have been tested over the years, but they are too tricky to steer and slow down.

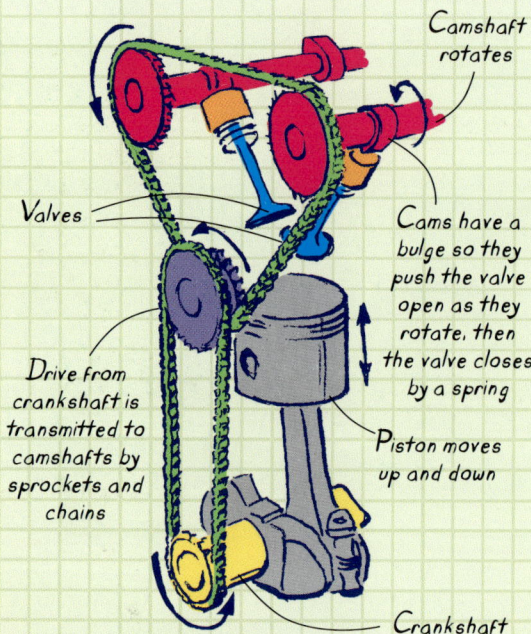

Some racing bike engines run at 18,000 rpm (revolutions per minute) – 300 times per second.

Lights

Camshaft rotates

Valves

Cams have a bulge so they push the valve open as they rotate, then the valve closes by a spring

Drive from crankshaft is transmitted to camshafts by sprockets and chains

Piston moves up and down

Crankshaft

Forks Hydraulic dampers and springs (shock absorbers) absorb road bumps and sudden steering manoeuvres.

How do DOHC ENGINES work?

A petrol or diesel engine has mushroom-shaped valves at the top of each cylinder. The inlet valve opens to let in fresh air and fuel mixture. When this mix has exploded, the exhaust valve opens to let out the stale gases. The valves open by being pushed downwards. In the double overhead camshaft (DOHC) each valve is pushed by a collar-like part with a bulge on one side, the 'cam'. This turns on an 'overhead' shaft spinning above the engine. There are two shafts, hence the word 'double'.

Brake disc Special metal alloys and plenty of ventilation holes prevent the disc overheating.

Spokes As few spokes as possible decrease wheel weight and air resistance as the wheel spins.

Visit www.factsforprojects.com and click on the web link to view pictures, read facts and watch videos of the Yamaha.

Handlebars The handlebars are set low down, so the rider crouches over them for less air resistance, rather than sitting more upright.

In a MotoGP race the rider who finishes first gains 25 points, the second rider receives 20, third place is 16, and so on — all the way down to the rider who comes in fifteenth, who gains one point!

Low-profile seat

Cleland rides into the record books on his electric superbike

✳ Going ELECTRIC

The problem with electric motorbikes is the great weight of the batteries. Not only do they slow down the vehicle and make it less efficient, they also cause difficulties with balance, since leaning over slightly means shifting their heavy weight and making the bike less steady. However record-breaking electric motorcycles only need enough current for a few runs. In 2009 Jeremy Cleland set a new electric motorbike top speed of 240 kilometres per hour.

Rear drive sprocket

MotoGP has several classes, including 125 cc and Moto2 (600 cc) for smaller-engined motorbikes, and the MotoGP class for bigger engines.

The fastest speed for a MotoGP bike was set in 2009 at 349.3 km/h by Dani Pedrosa on his Repsol Honda, during practise at the Italian Grand Prix.

Tyres Different tyre patterns and treads are used depending on conditions, with smooth 'slicks' in the dry and grooved treads when it is wet.

Engine The R1 has four cylinders in a line across the bike (left to right), each parallel to the others. The cylinders are forward-inclined, or leaning to the front. The total engine size is 998 cc (almost one litre).

Suspension arms The suspension design is known as swingarm. It has a long bar on each side that pivots at its front end, with the wheel at its rear end.

Until 1987, riders were allowed to push-start their MotoGP bikes and jump on when the engine was going!

9

NASCAR STOCK CAR

Stock racing cars are based on cars that anyone can buy from a normal supply or 'stock'. Of course the rules say that they can be souped up with more powerful engines, tougher suspension and better safety equipment. The world's biggest stock car races are organized by the US National Association for Stock Car Auto Racing, NASCAR, and draw giant crowds of 200,000 or more.

Eureka!

Racing 'modded' or modified ordinary cars on normal roads might seem cool. However over the years it's caused many tragedies. NASCAR had its origins in the first organized races during the 1930s and was founded in 1948.

Whatever next?

Most stock cars race on giant oval tracks called speedways, raceways or bowls. Speeds are limited not so much by the cars themselves, but by how tightly the track curves at the bends and other safety factors.

The longest NASCAR track is Talladega in Alabama, USA at 4.3 km.

* How do OHV ENGINES work?

The mushroom-shaped valves of a petrol or diesel engine open to allow fresh fuel-air mixture into the cylinder, and let out stale gases after the mixture has burned or combusted (see page 8). In the OHV or overhead valve design, the valves are in the top of the cylinder. Each one is opened by a see-saw rocker that is tilted from below by a long push rod. This is pushed up by a cam, which is like a ring with a bulge on one side. The cam turns on a spinning camshaft low down, beside the main engine.

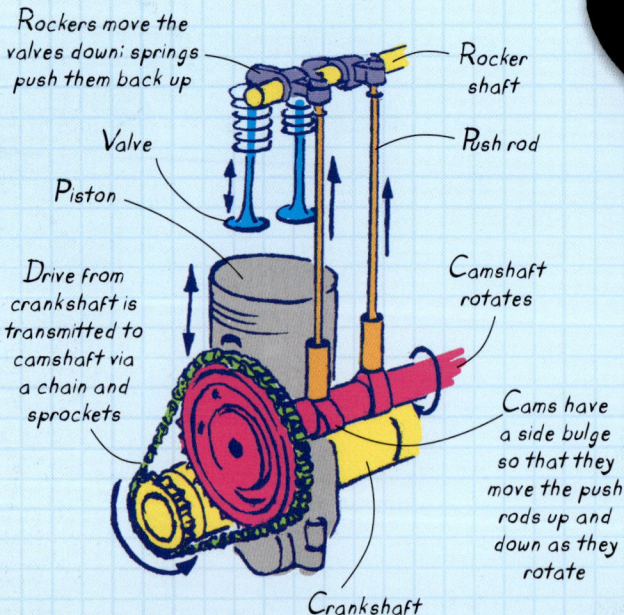

Rockers move the valves down; springs push them back up

Rocker shaft

Valve

Push rod

Piston

Drive from crankshaft is transmitted to camshaft via a chain and sprockets

Camshaft rotates

Cams have a side bulge so that they move the push rods up and down as they rotate

Crankshaft

Radiator The 'rad' is a very vulnerable part of the car. If damaged, its engine-cooling water leaks and the engine may overheat and even seize up completely.

V8 Engine The main NASCAR events specify an 8-cylinder engine of 5860 cc with pushrod valves (see below left).

Fan belt

Front skirt

Radiator

Sponsors Several sponsors provide money or equipment for the race teams. In return they gain publicity with their names and logos displayed on the cars and trackside.

Racing tyres To even out car performance, NASCAR entries use Goodyear slick tyres – that is, smooth, with no tread.

NASCAR drivers must wear a collar-like HANS (Head And Neck Support) to prevent neck injuries in high-speed impact.

Discover how NASCAR stock cars are made and raced by visiting www.factsforprojects.com and clicking on the web link.

NASCAR is a family concern. It was founded by Bill France Snr in 1948. In 2003 his grandson Brian France became chief of the organization.

Roll cage A strong cage of welded metal tubes stops the car and driver being crushed if the car rolls over in a serious crash. The tubes and weld joints must exceed a certain level of strength.

Of the World Top 20 crowds for single-day sports events, NASCAR draws more than 15 of the biggest.

Shatterproof windows The windows are made from special impact-resistant clear plastic.

Spoiler This angled surface 'spoils' the airflow at the rear of the car, giving a downward force that keeps the wheels pressed against the track.

Jimmie Johnston won his fourth successive NASCAR Sprint Cup title in 2009. No other driver has won four in a row.

Side skirt

Odd tyres The tyres can be different sizes depending on the direction and tightness of the track's bends.

NASCAR oval speedways evolved from races at Daytona Beach, Florida, with straight sections along the sand and the beachfront highway joined by two tight bends.

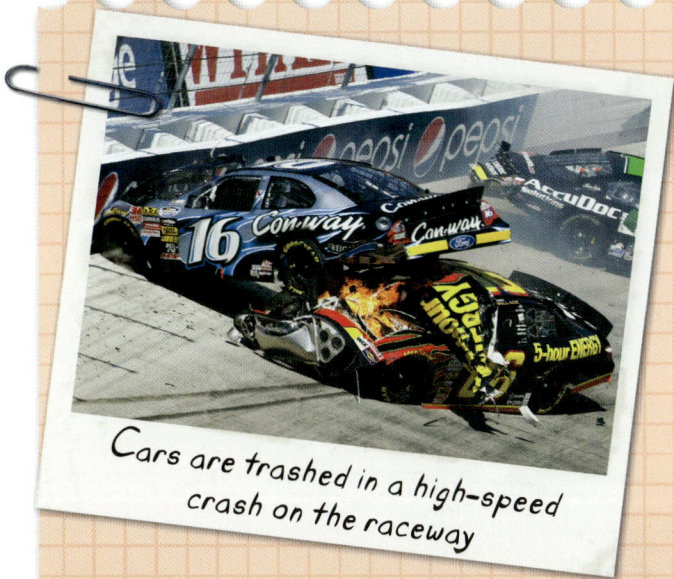

Cars are trashed in a high-speed crash on the raceway

✳ Rough 'n' TOUGH

Stock car racing is not just about speed. Drivers can swerve in front of each other, brake to slow down the car behind, and even nudge other cars out of the way, although all of the action is controlled by strict laws. Sometimes cars smash into the outer barrier around the track or get pushed onto the grassy infield at its centre. With speeds reaching 300-plus kilometres per hour, drivers need nerves of steel, and also plenty of aggression to force their way to the front and stay there.

MCLAREN F1 SUPERCAR

People who love fast cars like to think they are driving a vehicle that's just one step away from the very best on the track – Formula One Grand Prix. The McLaren F1 was produced during the 1990s as the ultimate road car, based on the McLaren team's fantastic record of Formula One successes. The driver has that 'F1' feel because unlike in other super sports cars, the two passenger seats on either side are set slightly behind the driver.

Eureka!

McLaren's aim was a car with very low weight, extremely high power, and high-tech parts and components 'borrowed' from Formula One. Only 106 F1s were built. They rarely come up for sale.

Whatever next?

In 1998, the F1 set a record 391 kilometres per hour for a production road car. Since then others have gone faster, more than 410 kilometres per hour.

The F1 has a six-speed manual gearbox – not automatic.

Butterfly doors The doors move both out and up as they open, so that people do not have to stoop down too low to get in.

✳ How does ABS work?

Anti-lock braking system, ABS, stops the road wheels 'locking' or stopping suddenly when the driver brakes too hard. It's safer if the wheels keep their grip on the road, rather than locking and skidding. Electronic sensors check the spinning speed of each wheel. If one starts to turn slower than the others, this indicates it could lock. So a valve in the brake pipe to that wheel reduces the brake pressure. This happens many times very fast, as a series of clicks or pulses.

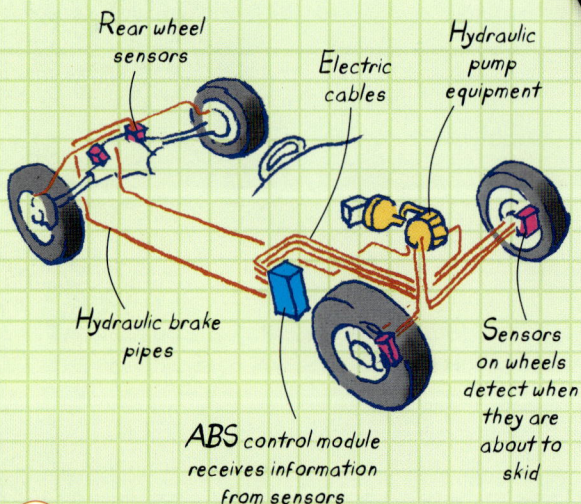

Radiator

Battery

Rear wheel sensors

Electric cables

Hydraulic pump equipment

Hydraulic brake pipes

ABS control module receives information from sensors

Sensors on wheels detect when they are about to skid

The F1 is 4.29 m long, 1.82 m wide and just 1.14 m high. Its fully fuelled weight is 1.14 tonnes.

Central driving position The driver sits in the centre of the vehicle, which gives much better weight distribution and stability than being to one side.

MICHELIN

For further facts and information on the McLaren F1
visit www.factsforprojects.com and click on the web link.

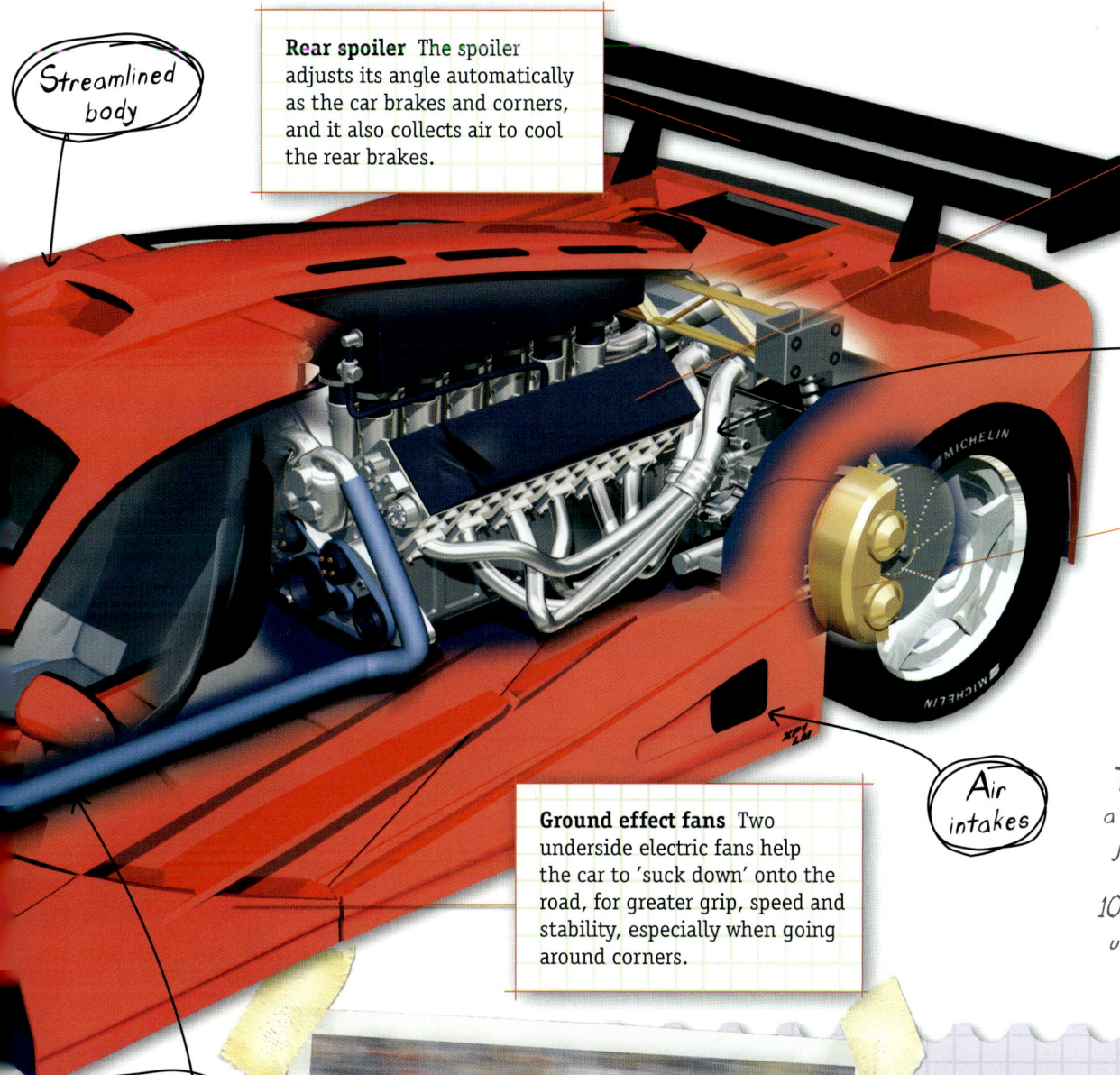

Streamlined body

Rear spoiler The spoiler adjusts its angle automatically as the car brakes and corners, and it also collects air to cool the rear brakes.

BMW V12 engine The 12-cylinder, 6.1-litre S70/2 engine produces 672 horsepower – over five times more than a typical family car.

Exhaust

Powerful brakes On the original F1 design the brakes were not power-assisted and there was no ABS (see left), but some of the cars have since been converted.

Air intakes

Ground effect fans Two underside electric fans help the car to 'suck down' onto the road, for greater grip, speed and stability, especially when going around corners.

The F1 accelerates from a standstill to 100 km/h in just over three seconds. It can then brake from 100 km/h to zero in slightly under three seconds and less than 40 m.

Engine cooling system

Two self-build kit cars called Edward and Albert were used as testbeds or 'mules' for various parts of the F1.

Although designed for the road, the F1 still triumphed on the track

✳ BACK on the TRACK

The McLaren F1 was designed as a 'street legal' road car. It has indicator lights, side lights and other features needed by law for normal roads, that track cars do not have. Yet it still managed to win several track races, including the world-famous gruelling Le Mans 24-Hour in France in 1995. The race-ready F1 was slightly changed from the normal road version, as it had to compete against cars purpose-designed and specially built for that particular race at the Le Mans circuit.

TESLA ROADSTER

Electric cars are nothing new. They have been around for more than 100 years. In fact in 1899 the world land speed record was held by an electric car (see below). With modern worries about the energy crisis, exhaust pollution and global warming, electric cars are making a comeback. There are some people at the traffic lights who always want to speed away faster than everyone else. The all-electric Tesla Roadster is ideal for them.

Eureka!

In the 1970s–80s, partly because of political problems around the world, there were worries about the supply of oil (petroleum) to make petrol and diesel. Coupled with new air pollution laws, people went back to the old idea of electric cars.

Whatever next?

The key to success with electric cars is better batteries that charge faster and power the vehicle for longer. Several new kinds of batteries offer hope for the future.

Lotus windscreen

Sports styling
Typically low, sleek sports-car styling based on the Lotus Elise gives the Roadster very low air resistance.

Body panels All body panels are made from carbon fibre composites, helping to keep the car's weight down to about 1.23 tonnes.

In a special endurance race a Roadster covered 511 km on a single charge.

✳ When VOLTS ruled

During the later 1800s, the newly invented petrol and diesel engines were still noisy and unreliable. Electric motors had been around for many years, and they powered various kinds of cars and wagons. In 1899 Belgian race ace Camille Jenatzy set a new land speed record in his electric car *La Jamais Contente* (meaning 'Never Satisfied'). On a straight road near Paris, France, it sped along at 105.9 kilometres per hour – the first land vehicle to go past 100 kilometres per hour.

The Roadster is very economical, covering about 50 km on the electrical energy equivalent of one litre of petrol.

Jenatzy celebrates his record in the electric La Jamais Contente

Choose your very own Tesla Roadster – exterior and interior colours – and watch it being built by visiting www.factsforprojects.com and clicking on the web link.

The Roadster's battery packs take about 3.5 hours for a full charge.

Lithium-ion batteries
The battery packs or 'ESS' (Energy Storage System) contain more than 6800 Li-ion cells arranged in separate sheets, which are cooled by a circulating fluid.

The Roadster is the first production electric car to travel more than 300 km on a single charge of electricity. In fact, driven carefully it can cover almost 400 km.

Electric circuits
Computerized electronics keep a check on the battery packs, motor and other circuits, and lessen power to the motor if there are problems.

The Roadster has excellent acceleration, going from zero to just under 100 km/h in 3.7 seconds. However some drivers say that it is too quiet. They like a car to roar as they speed away.

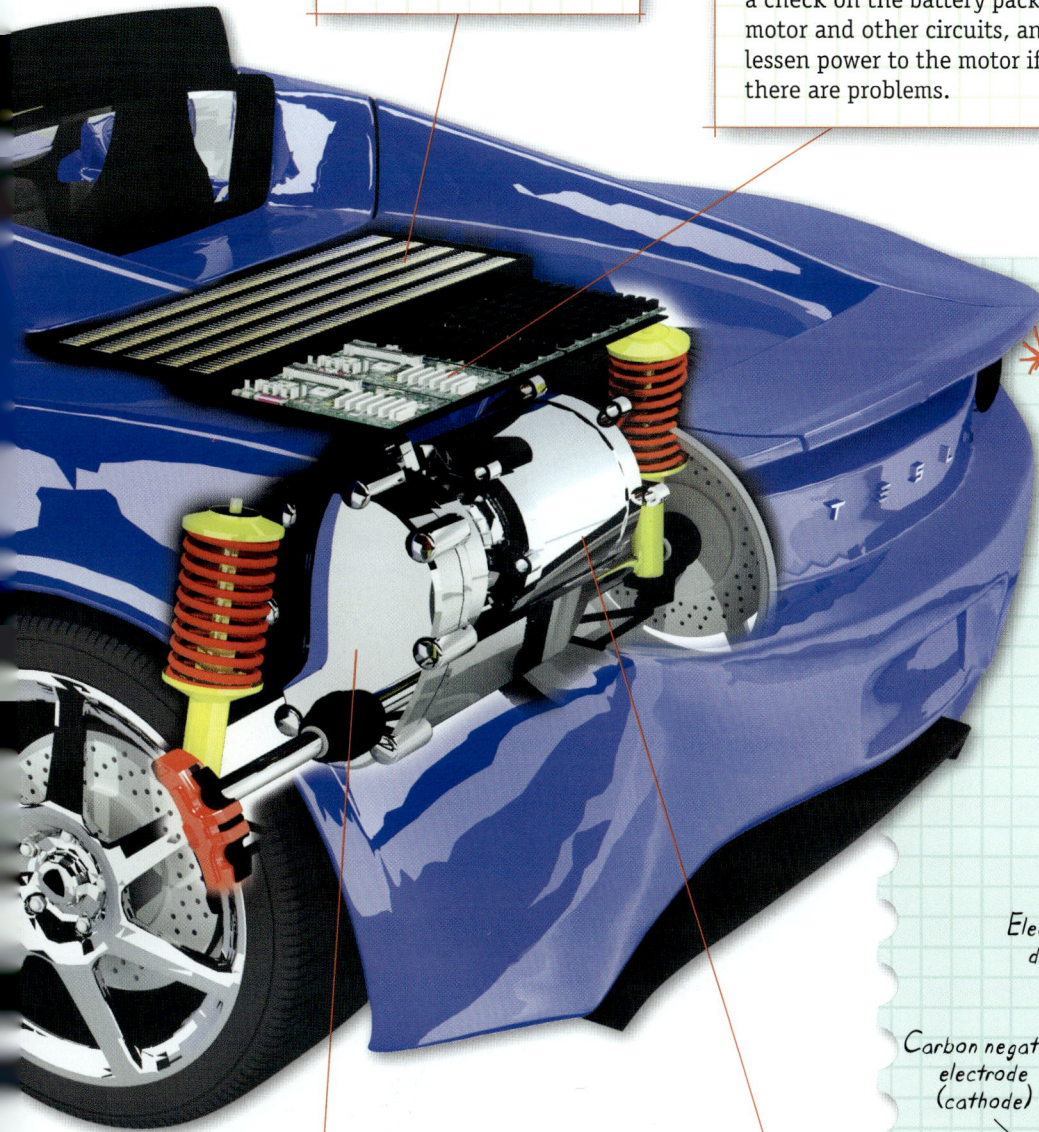

Electric motor The single electric motor weighs just 32 kilograms, yet in the Sports version of the Roadster it produces almost 290 horsepower. It spins more than 10,000 times each minute at high speed.

Transmission Because electric motors have a powerful turning force (torque) throughout their speed range, there are no gears to change – the gearbox is single-speed.

How do LI-ION CELLS work?

Lithium-ion rechargeable batteries are found in all kinds of gadgets, from mp3 players and mobile phones to laptops. The Li-ion battery is a group of individual Li-ion cells. When the battery is charged, particles called lithium ions, which are positive, are forced to move from the negative contact (cathode) to the positive one (anode). When in use (see diagram below), the ions naturally go back, attracted to the negative contact, and their movement forms an electric current.

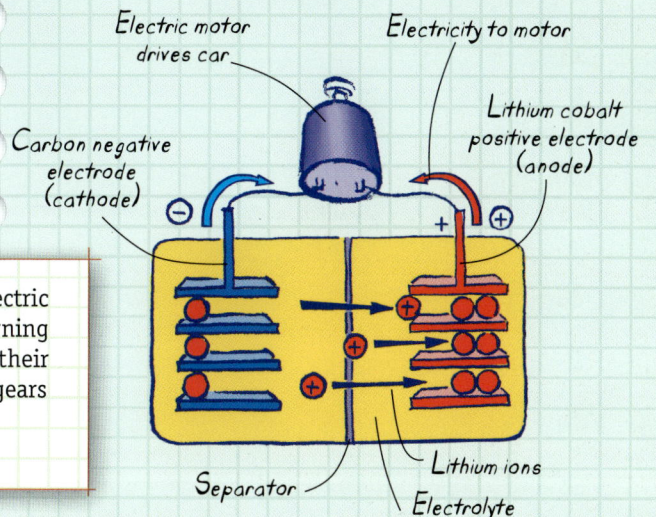

Electric motor drives car

Electricity to motor

Carbon negative electrode (cathode)

Lithium cobalt positive electrode (anode)

Separator

Lithium ions

Electrolyte

BLUEBIRD CN7

Some people say that speed and risk-taking run in the family. This was certainly true of Malcolm Campbell and his son Donald. The father set 13 world speed records in cars and boats during the 1920s–30s, and son Donald continued the tradition in the 1950s–60s (see page 22). The name *Bluebird* was used for many of their vehicles. In *Bluebird CN7* Donald took the land speed record in 1964 at 648.7 kilometres per hour.

Eureka!

At first, world speed records had no official rules or independent timekeepers. In 1904 the FIA (Fédération Internationale de Automobile) formed in Paris, to oversee all kinds of car racing and also land speed record attempts.

The first version of *Bluebird CN7* lacked a vertical stabilizer or tail fin. This unusual design could have contributed to its crash at Bonneville in 1960.

The 'C' in CN7 refers to Donald Campbell. The 'N' is for the Norris brothers, Ken and Lew, who carried out most of the design work on Campbell's cars and boats.

Aeroweb bodywork The smoothly curved body had outer and inner skins of very thin metal alloy separated by a sponge-like layer of 20-mm-thick metal 'honeycomb'.

Cockpit The driver's cockpit was smoothed into the front of the car, The steering wheel in the cockpit was linked to the steering mechanism between the front wheels by two chains.

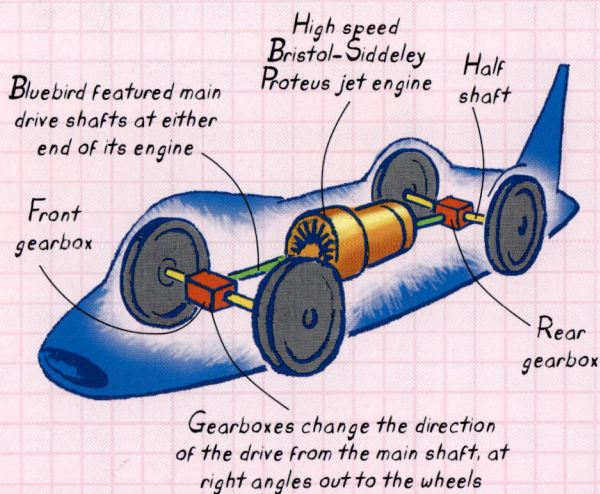

Wheel fairing

High speed Bristol-Siddeley Proteus jet engine

Half shaft

Bluebird featured main drive shafts at either end of its engine

Front gearbox

Rear gearbox

Gearboxes change the direction of the drive from the main shaft, at right angles out to the wheels

✳ How do GEARBOXES work?

A gearbox has two or more wheels with teeth, called cogs, that fit or mesh together. A bigger cog turning a smaller cog makes the smaller cog spin much faster, but with less turning force or torque. A small cog meshing with a big one spins the big one more slowly but with more torque (turning force). The comparison between the cog sizes is called the gear ratio. The trick is to get the best ratio for each gearbox. *Bluebird CN7*'s designers did many calculations and experiments to get the best ratio between the spinning speed of the engine and the road wheels.

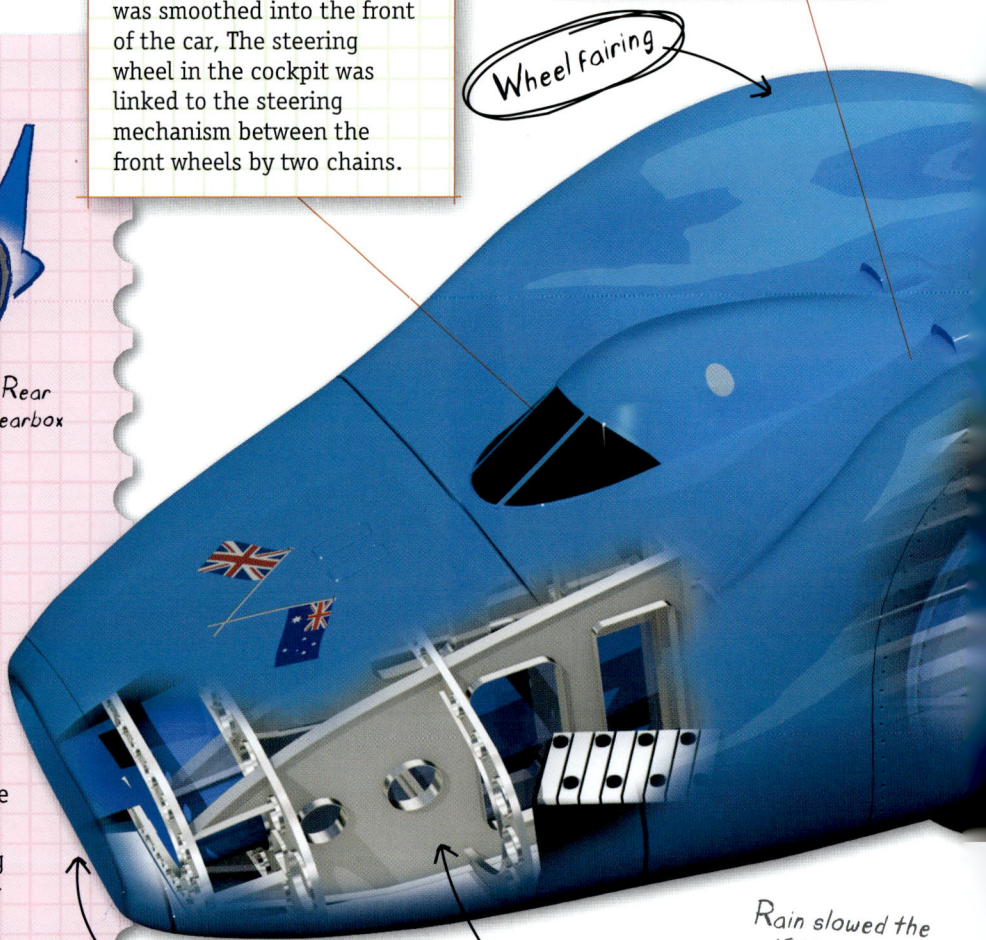

Aircraft-type construction

Air intake

Rain slowed the 1964 record-breaking run at Lake Eyrie. Campbell had expected to reach 700 km/h.

Learn more about racing legends Malcolm and Donald Campbell by visiting www.factsforprojects.com and clicking the web link.

In the 1960 Bonneville crash, CN7 took off for more than 300 m and bounced three times.

Chassis The main chassis (framework) was constructed of aluminium-based alloys for strength and extreme lightness, with a hoop-like design similar to an aircraft fuselage.

Fin (vertical stabilizer) This upright surface helped to prevent the CN7 swerving from side to side or 'snaking' at high speed.

Bristol-Siddeley Proteus engine Designed for aircraft use, this 5000-horsepower jet engine delivered its power by spinning a drive shaft, rather than by blasting a thrust of hot gases from the rear exhaust.

Four Proteus engines were also used to drive the propellers on the huge Bristol Britannia airliner of the 1950s–60s.

Dunlop tyres Specially made tyres with an outer diameter of 1.32 metres and width of 20 centimetres were fitted to the lightweight alloy metal disc wheels.

Fuel tanks

Oxygen bottles

Brakes The CN7 had three separate braking systems, including disc brakes on the inner sides of the wheel and air brakes at the rear.

✳ Always in DANGER

Speed record attempts are always dangerous. On land, you need the longest, flattest place on Earth. This is usually the dried-up bottom of a salt lake, where the slowly drying water leaves behind a hard, flat sheet or bed of salt crystals. The first *Bluebird CN7* was wrecked in 1960 in a crash at Bonneville Salt Flats in the USA. The next version went to Lake Eyrie in Australia but its 1963 attempt was washed out by the first rain there in 20 years.

The wrecked first Bluebird CN7 after its high-speed crash

THRUST SSC

In 1997 at Black Rock Desert, Nevada, USA, there was a huge roaring noise and then an eerie thunder-like boom. It was the first land vehicle to go faster than sound and break the 'sound barrier' – jet-powered *Thrust* SSC (SuperSonic Car). Driven by jet fighter pilot Andy Green, it clocked an average speed over two runs of 1228 kilometres per hour.

Eureka!

The land speed record shift from petrol engines to jets began in the 1960s. At first the official rules did not recognize jet cars. But after much argument they agreed that there should be several types of record. The 'absolute' one has been held by jets ever since.

Whatever next?

Several teams are building cars to break *Thrust SSC*'s record, including the UK's *Bloodhound* project and the US-Canada *North American Eagle*.

Thrust SSC's two jet engines had a power output of 110,000 horsepower.

More than 100 electronic sensors sent information by radio to the pit crew.

Driver Andy Green kept in touch with the pit crew, who informed him when to hit maximum power in order to pass the timing equipment at top speed.

Thrust SSC makes its record-breaking run

Air intake

Girder chassis

The total length of *Thrust*'s run track was almost 20 km.

✳ Rules RULE!

The official land speed record rules say that a vehicle must be timed as it goes between two points a certain distance apart, twice – usually on one day and then the next. The two runs or passes can be in the same direction. Formerly they had to be in opposite directions, within an hour of each other – this is how *Thrust SSC* gained its record. The rules mean the vehicle needs several kilometres to get up speed. Then the driver must get to top speed and stay there as the vehicle passes the timing equipment. There should also be enough distance after the measurement to slow down safely.

Nose cone The streamlining of *Thrust* SSC included an almost needle-sharp nose, which contained a crash sensor that set off the automatic fire extinguisher.

Engine pod Each engine was about 5.2 metres long and one metre in diameter, with a weight of almost two tonnes.

Watch an amazing video of Thrust SSC in action by visiting
www.factsforprojects.com and clicking on the web link.

The two engines would burn the amount of jet fuel equivalent to a family car's full tank of petrol in three seconds.

Steering The two offset rear wheels, one in front and slightly to the side of the other, steered the vehicle.

Fuel tank More than 1000 litres of jet fuel were used for each run, contained in the specially constructed fireproof tank.

Tailplane

How does PARACHUTE BRAKING work?

The fastest land vehicles go so quickly that when they try to slow down, even special brakes would glow red hot within a second or two. Instead the driver releases a small umbrella-shaped parachute from the rear. This is the drogue, which catches the air and pulls out the much bigger main parachute for greater air resistance. Once the speed has dropped enough, the driver can then apply the brakes.

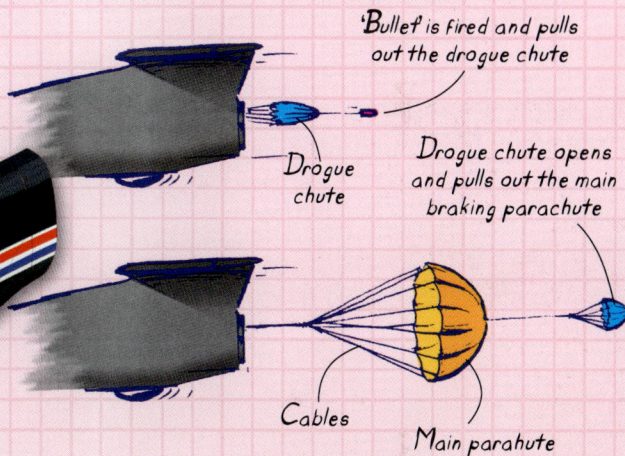

'Bullet' is fired and pulls out the drogue chute

Drogue chute

Drogue chute opens and pulls out the main braking parachute

Cables

Main parahute

Rolls-Royce Spey jet engines After early tests with the Spey 202, the engines were updated to the Spey 205 version. These engines have powered many aircraft, from Buccaneer and Phantom fighters to the BAC 111 jetliner and Nimrod military reconnaissance craft.

Formers Each engine was encased in a metal tube with a framework of hoop-like formers.

Engine cowl

Thrust had six carbon wheel brakes, two for each front wheel and one for each rear wheel.

Front wheels Since SSC was driven by thrust from the jet engines, the front and rear wheels simply rotated by themselves. All wheels are solid aluminium discs without tyres.

Thrust SSC is 16.5 m long and weighs more than 10 tonnes when ready to go. This compares to a length of just over 9 m and a weight of 4.2 tonnes for its record-holding predecessor from 1964, Bluebird CN7 (see page 16).

TGV BULLET TRAIN

The speediest trains are long, slim and extra-streamlined, with a rounded front, similar to a bullet. They travel almost as fast as real bullets fired from guns. One type is the French TGV, *Train a Grande Vitesse* ('Big Speed Train'). The locomotive or pulling part has huge electric motors that are powered by electric current gathered from overhead wires. On a special test run in 2007 a TGV took the world rail speed record at 574.8 kilometres per hour.

Eureka!

There are many kinds of passenger-carrying electric trains, from subway types in tunnels below cities, to specialized services in big airports and shopping malls. The first ones operated in 1879 at the Berlin Trade Fair, Germany.

Whatever next?

Train speeds continue to increase. A recent record for the fastest regular passenger service was set by the Harmony Express in China. at speeds of more than 310 kilometres per hour.

'Shinkansen' means 'New Main Line' in Japanese.

Cooling The electrical equipment in the power or traction car has its own cooling systems and hot-air vents.

Driver's cab The driver keeps in touch by radio with other on-board staff as well as with signallers and track controllers.

Polarized glass

SNCF

Power car

Motorized bogie The front bogies have wheels turned by powerful electric motors next to them.

A Japanese bullet train waiting at the station

✳ JAPANESE BULLETS

The original 'bullet trains' were Japanese Shinkansens, which came into service in 1964. Every few years newer, faster versions or series are introduced. They take many years of design and testing so that they are safe and reliable. The Shinkansen E5 series trains are designed to travel at speeds of up to 320 kilometres per hour. They could probably go faster still. But there are other limitations such as wear on the overhead lines, too much noise outside and inside, and trains taking too long to slow down.

The first Japanese bullet trains reached speeds of 200 km/h. Newer test versions have reached 440 km/h. Several countries now have high-speed networks, such as AVE in Spain and THSR in Taiwan.

Watch a video of the fastest rail train setting the world record by visiting www.factsforprojects.com and clicking on the web link.

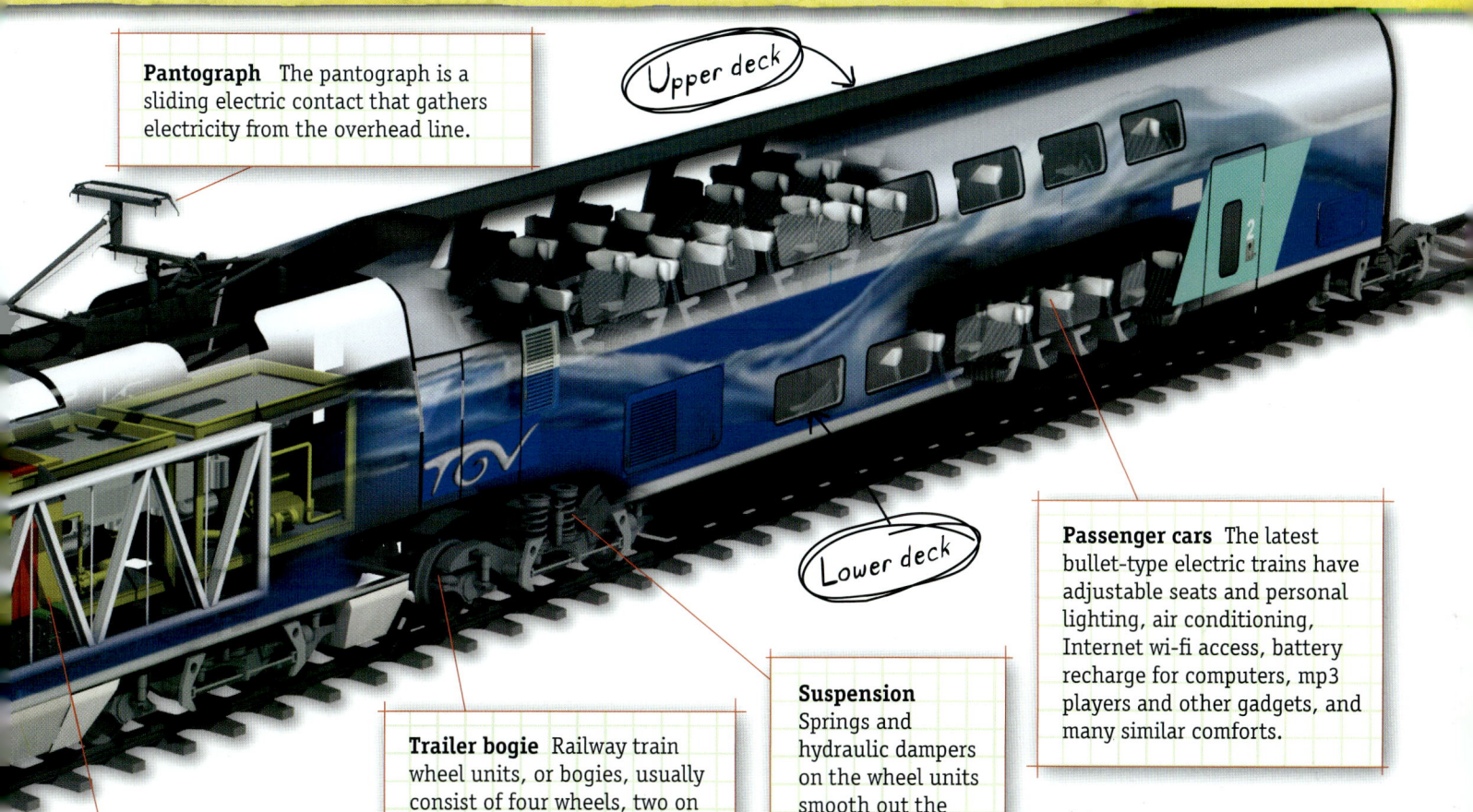

Pantograph The pantograph is a sliding electric contact that gathers electricity from the overhead line.

Upper deck

Lower deck

Passenger cars The latest bullet-type electric trains have adjustable seats and personal lighting, air conditioning, Internet wi-fi access, battery recharge for computers, mp3 players and other gadgets, and many similar comforts.

Suspension Springs and hydraulic dampers on the wheel units smooth out the ups and downs of the track.

Electrics The power car is mostly filled with huge power packs and transformers to change the very high voltage of the overhead current into a voltage suitable for the wheel motors.

Trailer bogie Railway train wheel units, or bogies, usually consist of four wheels, two on each side. The whole bogie can swing or steer to the left or right as the track curves. The trailer bogies are unpowered, with no electric motors.

Compared to more than 500 km/h for electric trains, the fastest steam locomotive was Mallard, reaching 202 km/h in 1938.

Maglev trains have no wheels or any other contact with the track. The cars are held up and moved by very strong magnetic forces. Manned maglev trains in Japan have exceeded 580 km/h on the Yamanashi Test Track near Kofu.

The fastest ever rail speed was set by a rocket-powered 'sledge' that reached more than 10,000 km/h – with no person on board. This happened as part of weapons safety testing in 2003 at Holloman Air Force Base in New Mexico, USA.

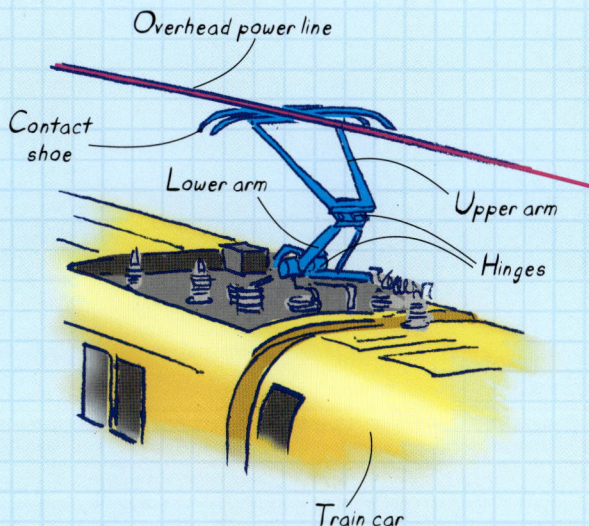

Overhead power line

Contact shoe

Lower arm

Upper arm

Hinges

Train car

✳ How does a PANTOGRAPH work?

The pantograph is a hinged arm that holds up an electrical contact against the overhead wire or cable, for an electric train, tram or trolleybus. It is spring-loaded, or it has hydraulic or pneumatic pistons, to keep it pressed against the wire with the right amount of force. Too little pressure means that the contact shoe flops and bounces, causing sparks and loss of power. Too much pressure and the shoe and wire wear away fast.

BLUEBIRD K7

In 1964 British speed expert Donald Campbell set both the world land and water speed records (see page 16). This itself is a record – no one else has achieved the double. Campbell's watercraft, like his cars, were called *Bluebird*. Between 1955 and 1964 in the jet-powered *Bluebird K7* he set the water speed record seven times. After a new jet engine was fitted, he tried to go even faster in 1967. But the craft crashed at great speed and Campbell was killed.

Eureka!

Bluebird K7 was one of the first of a new breed of jet-powered speedboats. Before the mid 1950s, most record-holders were propeller-driven craft with petrol or diesel engines. Recently there have also been rocket-powered boats, but jet power still rules (see page 24).

Whatever next?

A major problem for speedboats is waves. Even the smallest ripple can cause the craft to flip over. Special environmentally-safe chemicals on the water could make it smoother.

Stabilizing fin The upright fin helped to keep the craft aiming straight. It was adapted from the same aircraft that the engine comes from, the Folland Gnat jet trainer.

Bristol Siddeley Orpheus jet engine After six records with a Metropolitan Vickers Beryl engine, K7 was fitted with a more powerful Orpheus that was 2.4 metres long and weighed 440 kilograms.

Transparent sponson fin

Water rudders At first the rudder area was too large, causing the craft to swerve violently at speed. The design was 'offset' – not based on the centreline along the middle of the boat but slightly to one side.

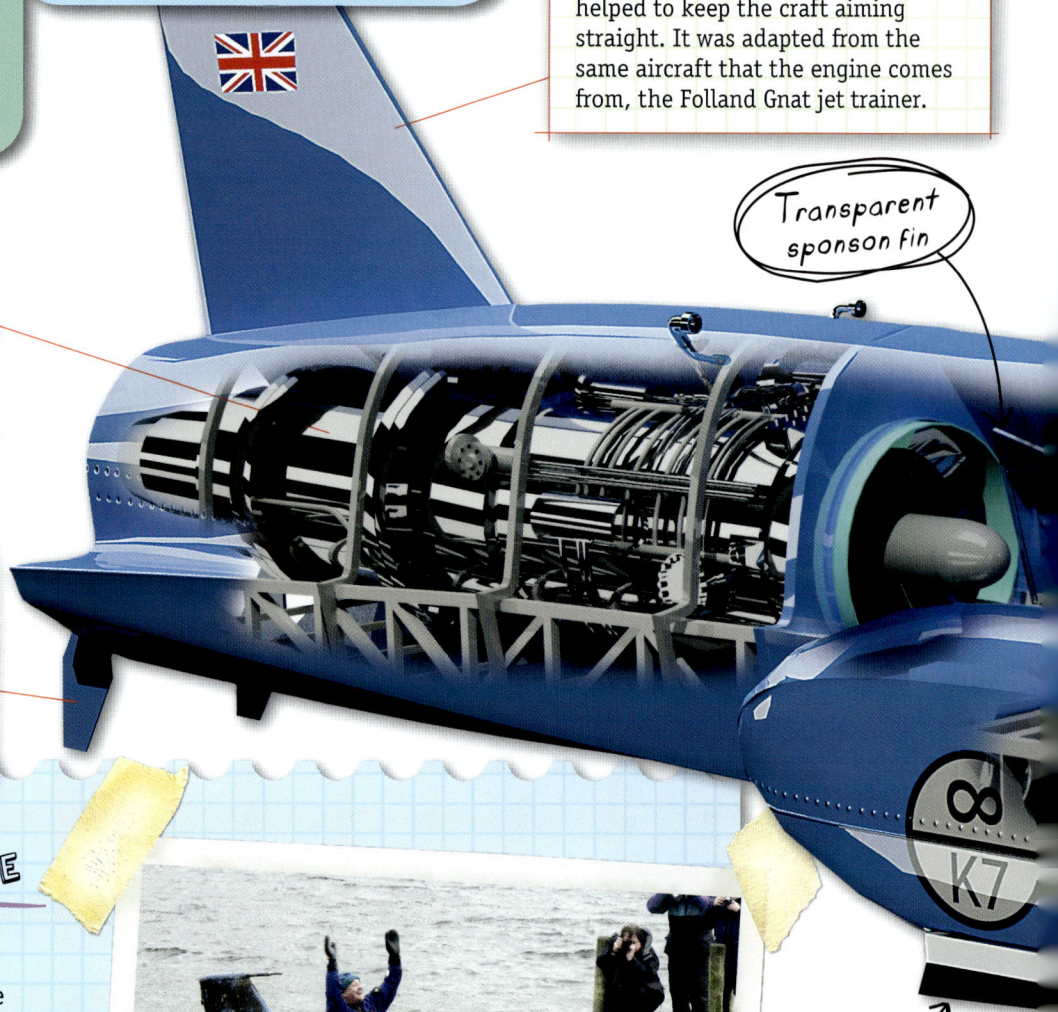

✳ Back to the SURFACE

Campbell's final water record attempt was at Coniston Water in the Lake District, northwest England. After the crash at more than 480 kilometres per hour, many people thought that Campbell's body and craft should be left on the lake bed, as a silent memorial. During 2000–01 divers recovered them, so that Campbell could be given a suitable burial and the craft could be examined to see what went wrong. There was still fuel in the pipe to the engine, so the idea that the fuel ran out may not be correct.

Sub-sponson fin

K7 was 8 m long, 1.4 m high and weighed 2.5 tonnes.

After more than 30 years underwater, Bluebird K7 is recovered

Learn about the restoration of Bluebird K7 by visiting www.factsforprojects.com and clicking on the web link.

Campbell set his final water speed record in 1964, reaching 444.7km/h on Dumbleyung Lake, a 13-km long salt lake in Western Australia.

How does HYDROPLANING work?

Ordinary boats float in, not on, the water and so have to push through it as they move. Water is very heavy and moving through it needs massive energy. In hydroplaning (see page 24) the craft makes its own lifting force at speed and skims across the surface, which uses far less energy. The underside surfaces are specially shaped and spaced out to cause the craft to bounce back slightly each time it comes into contact with the water.

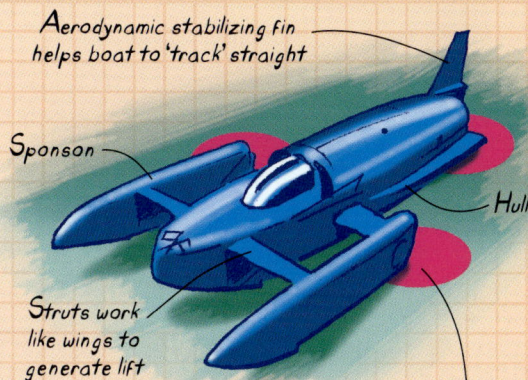

Aerodynamic stabilizing fin helps boat to 'track' straight

Sponson

Hull

Struts work like wings to generate lift

As Bluebird travels at high speed only three points are in contact the water - the rear tips of the sponsons and the rear of the main hull

Radio aerial

Cockpit The pilot needed good all-round frontal vision in order to avoid areas of ripples or waves. The see-through upright fin on each sponson allowed a clear view to the side.

Instrument panel

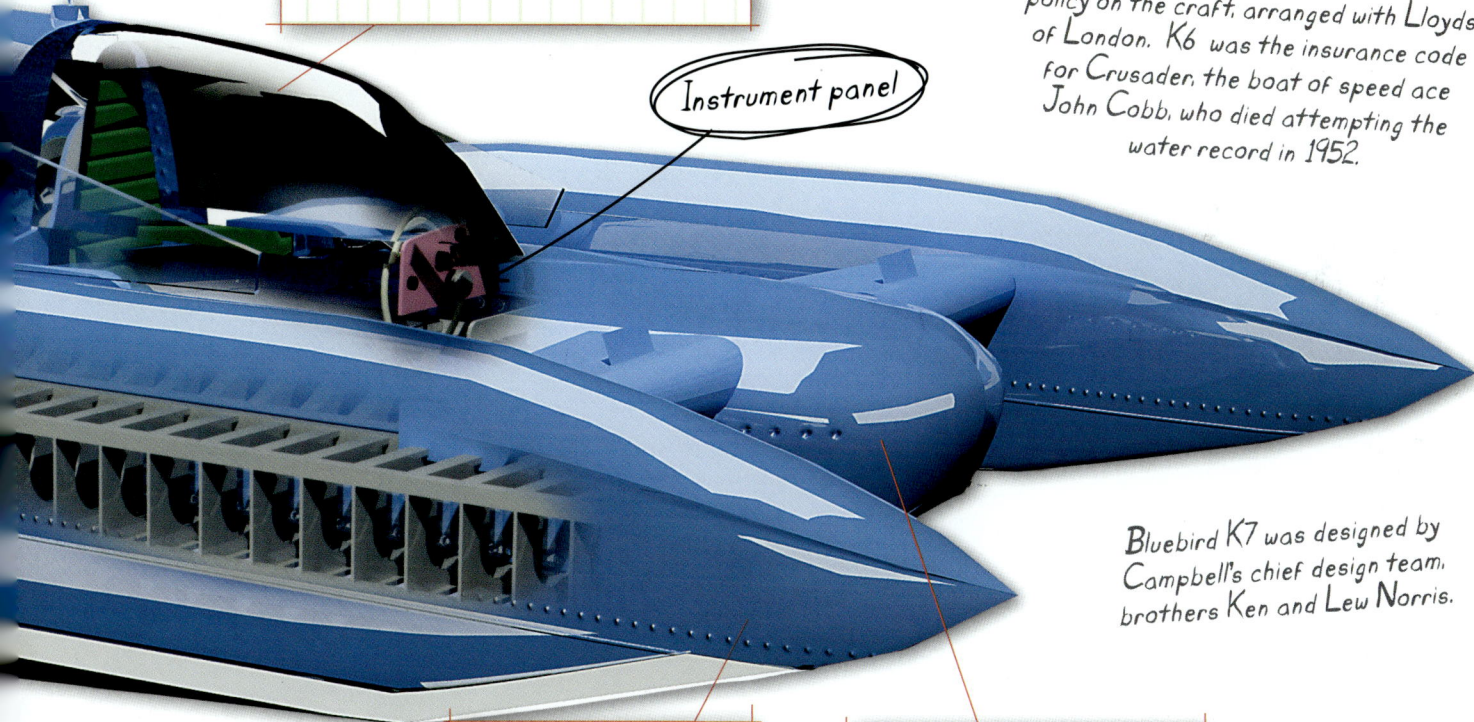

K7 is the code for the type of insurance policy on the craft, arranged with Lloyds of London. K6 was the insurance code for Crusader, the boat of speed ace John Cobb, who died attempting the water record in 1952.

Bluebird K7 was designed by Campbell's chief design team, brothers Ken and Lew Norris.

In 2009, K7's rescue team announced that the restored craft would race one more time on Coniston Water, as a tribute to Donald Campbell, before being put on museum display.

Sponsons These are like mini hulls on the side of the main hull, added to make the craft more stable and also to help it reach higher speed. Most very fast watercraft have a sponson design.

Main hull The main hull had a framework of high-strength steel tubes covered with body panels constructed of 'Birmabright' aluminium-magnesium lightweight alloy sheets.

The jet engine drank almost one litre of kerosene fuel per second and also sucked in 50 kg of air each second to burn it.

SPIRIT OF AUSTRALIA

No speed record has remained unbroken for so long as the fastest manned craft on water. It was set back in 1978 on Blowering Dam in southeast Australia. Boat pilot Ken Warby steered his jet-powered *Spirit of Australia* to an amazing 511 kilometres per hour. Everything was just right: the craft itself, its engine, the wind, the water surface and the pilot's skill. No other speed record has had so many failed attempts ending in tragedy, either. Several people have died trying to go faster than Warby.

Eureka!

Hydroplaning was discovered in the 1950s by speedboat designers tryng to improve their craft. They used ideas from aircraft design to make their craft 'fly' across the surface of the water rather than push through it (see page 23). The basic planing method has hardly changed since.

Whatever next?

Despite the dangers and warnings, speed-lovers still attempt the water speed record. Some are designing rocket-powered boats rather than using a jet engine.

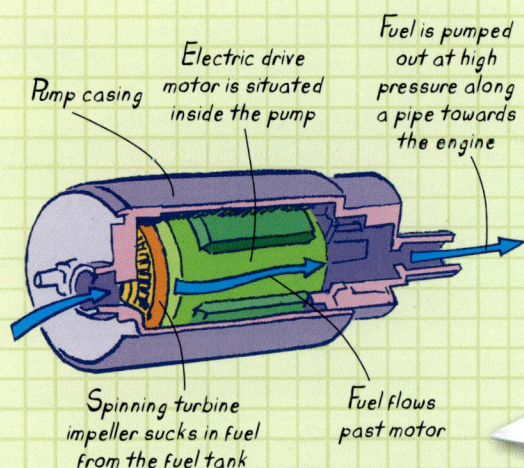

Hull cross-section

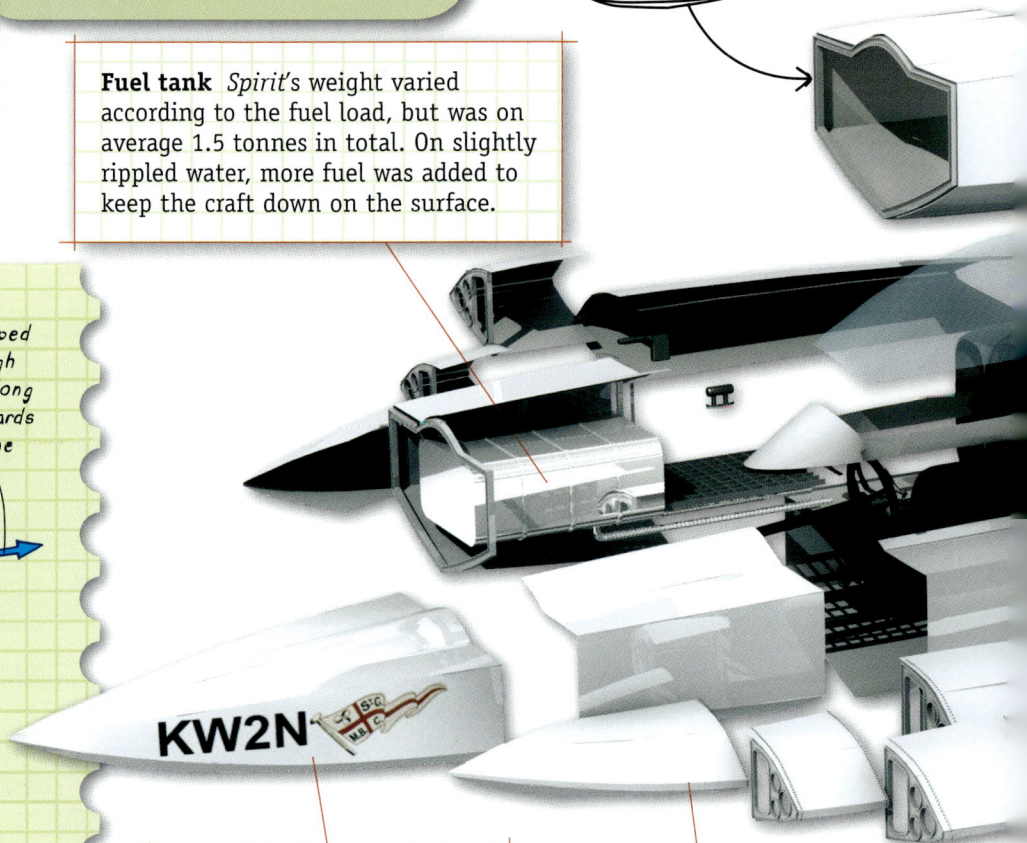

Fuel tank *Spirit*'s weight varied according to the fuel load, but was on average 1.5 tonnes in total. On slightly rippled water, more fuel was added to keep the craft down on the surface.

Pump casing

Electric drive motor is situated inside the pump

Fuel is pumped out at high pressure along a pipe towards the engine

Spinning turbine impeller sucks in fuel from the fuel tank

Fuel flows past motor

✴ How do FUEL PUMPS work?

Powerful jet engines need massive amounts of fuel. If the fuel pump fails, the engine suffers fuel starvation and this could cause a disaster. There are several designs for fuel pumps, including piston-based ones that squirt out fuel with each push of the piston. In another type an electric motor is actually inside the pump casing. It spins an impeller, like a rotating electric cooling fan with angled blades. The impeller sucks in fuel from the tank and pushes it at high speed and pressure into the engine.

KW2N

Main hull Spirit was just 8.2 metres long – tiny in comparison to many other rivals for the water speed record. Its hull was built not of complex metal alloys, but from a timber frame of spruce and Douglas fir trees, covered by plywood and fibreglass sheets.

Sponsons *Spirit of Australia* was of forward three-point design. It had the sponsons on either side at the front, with the hull touching the water at the rear.

Spirit, like many ultimate speed machines, is now in a museum – in this case the Australian National Maritime Museum in Darling Harbour, Sydney, Australia. The Museum also has one of Warby's balsawood models of Spirit, vital for testing in a wind tunnel.

Read lots of fascinating facts about the world land and water speed record-holders by visiting www.factsforprojects.com and clicking on the web link.

Tailplane Like the engine cowling, the tailplane was made of aluminium. Its angle was critical and adjusted many times to keep the rear of the boat pressed to the surface.

Warby and Spirit worked their way up to the world record with eight sets of runs between 1974 and 1978, first taking the world record in 1977 at 464 km/h.

Westinghouse J34 jet engine Rated at 6000 horsepower, the J34 turbojet has powered more than 20 different aircraft.

Engine cowling Because the jet engine got so hot, its shaped cover or cowling was made of aluminium sheet rather than plywood.

Canopy

At the end of one run Spirit was travelling at a maximum speed of 655 km/h.

SPIRIT OF AUSTRALIA
THE WORLD'S FASTEST BOAT

Fuel and turbine Fuel has to be forced into the jet engine's combustion chamber at the rate of more than one litre every second. The engine's turbine shaft rotated 12,500 times each minute.

FOSSE YS

Sponson skins

When Warby was building Spirit in his yard, he simply put a tarpaulin sheet over it to protect it from the rain.

Spirit of Australia in action

✳ New SPIRIT?

Ken Warby designed and built *Spirit of Australia* at home in his backyard. He bought the jet engine second-hand and got engineer friends from the local air force base to help him get it working again and install it in the craft. After the record, Warby took a rest from fast boats. But then he decided to try and break his own record by building another one, *Aussie Spirit*. It was similar to *Spirit* with a more powerful jet engine. However in 2007, after four years of testing, Warby decided to retire from the world water speed quest.

B-29 SUPERFORTRESS

Today, jet- and rocket-powered planes are the fastest craft in the air. But before jets were invented, designers pushed propeller power to its limits. One of the speediest and biggest 'prop' planes was the Boeing B-29 Superfortress, a heavy bomber in the US Air Force. Despite its huge weight of up to 60 tonnes, it could power along at top speeds of more than 570 kilometres per hour.

Eureka!

The B-29 had many high-tech features for its time. One was a pressurized cabin (see below). This idea was suggested in the 1920s. In 1931 the German Ju 49, a two-person, single-engined plane successfully tested the technology.

Whatever next?

In some ways, military aircraft no longer need to go faster and faster. They cannot easily outrun the fastest rocket missiles. More important is stealth – staying undetected by the enemy.

Pressurized tunnel A long tunnel linked the pressurized flight deck and nose section with the tail section. The main bomb bays could not be pressurized since their doors had to open.

Gun aimer's dome

Flight deck Up to six people were on the flight deck, including the pilot, co-pilot and flight engineer.

Norden bomb sight

Bomb bays The standard payload carried in the two huge bomb bays was 9 tonnes of various high explosives.

Hamilton propellers Built by the famous Hamilton engineering company, the four-bladed propellers were 5 metres across and when taxiing cleared the ground by only 36 centimetres.

✳ How does PRESSURIZATION work?

The higher you go, the colder it gets. Also there is less air, and so less oxygen for breathing. So early aircraft had to stay low, otherwise the people inside them would freeze and suffocate. However greater height takes an aircraft 'above the weather' and the thin air means it can go faster with less fuel. So a modern aircraft cabin is sealed and filled with warm air to keep people comfortable, known as cabin pressurization. The first passenger planes with this feature were the Boeing 307 (1938) and Lockheed Constellation (1943).

Entire cabin is a sealed unit that is heated and pressurized

At high altitude the air outside is freezing, has a lower pressure and is difficult to breathe

Main engines drive pumps to pressurize the cabin

On some aircraft the baggage compartment is not pressurized

Watch a video of the deadly B-29 in action by visiting www.factsforprojects.com and clicking on the web link.

Remote controlled turrets
The four remote turrets were aimed and fired by gunners in the nose and tail pressurized sections, using an early form of computerized remote control. Each turret had two M2 .50 calibre machine guns.

Fin

Rudder

Once airborne, the B-29 could fly and land with just two working engines.

Because of its pressurized conditions, the B-29 could fly at heights above 10,000 m – too high for most enemy fighter planes and anti-aircraft guns.

224863

Tail gunner The gunner in the rear turret was helped by an early form of radar-assisted aiming.

Tail skid

The B-29 was 30.1 m long, 8.5 m high and had a wingspan of 43 m. Its cruising speed was 350 km/h. Fully loaded with weapons its range was more than 5000 km.

Bunks

Engines In early B-29s the Wright R-3350 engines struggled for power and sometimes overheated. They were replaced by Pratt & Whitney R-4360s, each with 28 cylinders, producing 4300 horsepower.

Wing ribs

The name 'Superfortress' came about because the B-29 was developed from the earlier Boeing B-17 bomber nicknamed the 'Flying Fortress' because of its many defensive guns and weapons.

B-29s empty their deadly payload over Japan

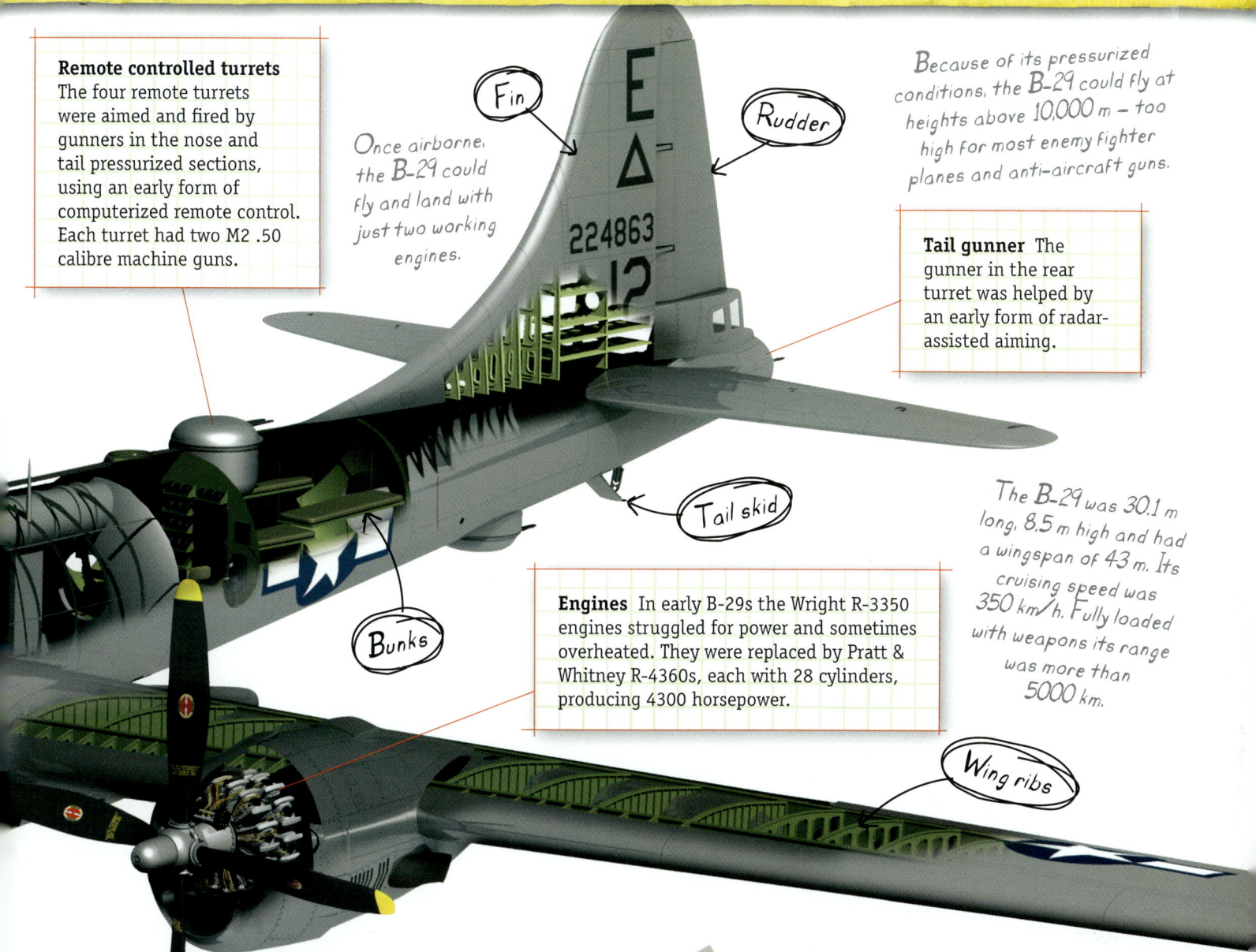

✳ An end to the WAR

B-29s were designed for long-range bombing raids, at first by day, and then at night too. After World War II (1939–45) finished in Europe, the battle against Japan continued. In the end the USA, Britain and other Allied Nations decided to use the ultimate weapon – the atomic bomb. The first was dropped over the city of Hiroshima, Japan on 6 August 1945, by a B-29 code-named *Enola Gay*. Three days later another bomb was dopped on the city of Nagasaki by the B-29 *Bockscar*. World War II ended soon afterwards.

LYNX HELICOPTER

Helicopters are not really built for speed. They have other special features, such as being able to take off and land straight up and down, hover in mid-air and even fly backwards. But speed comes in useful now and again, such as when rushing sick people to hospital in an air ambulance. In 1986 a Lynx helicopter set the world record for the fastest helicopter, at 401 kilometres per hour. The record still stands today.

Eureka!

Early helicopters were rattling machines that flew slowly and unsteadily. During the 1950s more powerful engines and better controls made them more agile in the air. One of the most successful was the Bell UH-1 (utility helicopter 1), called the 'Huey'.

Whatever next?

Helicopter racing is very skilled. Pilots race between one landing site and the next, land on a small target and even fly through hoops. Luckily these are small remote-controlled helicopters – at present.

Tail rotor The tail rotor steers the helicopter by counteracting the tendency of the main body to spin in the opposite direction to the main rotors.

Engines Power comes from two Rolls Royce Gem turboshaft engines, each producing 1000 horsepower.

Fin

The Westland Lynx first flew in 1971. After many trials it entered active military service in 1978. About 30 years later it is still in production, as the Agusta-Westland Lynx.

The Lynx and the improved Super Lynx are in service with almost 20 countries around the world, mainly as naval aircraft.

Tail skid

Tail boom The tail boom is lightweight and hollow, containing only the control and electrical cables for the tail rotor.

Two Lynx helicopters give an amazing display of airborne agility

*Aerial BALLET

Fast, agile helicopters like the Lynx work at the edge of their abilities. Turning sharply puts enormous stress on the mechanical parts, especially the whirling rotor blades and the rotor hub where they meet, because there are no fixed wings to take most of the strain. Even so, pilots have learnt to do all kinds of amazing aerobatics. In helicopters such as the Lynx and Apache they can even fly up and over in a circle or loop.

British forces have more than 200 Lynxes in service.

Take a virtual tour of a Lynx helicopter by visiting www.factsforprojects.com and clicking on the web link.

The Super Lynx, introduced in the 1990s, has a top speed of 325 km/h and can fly for 520 km unless equipped with extra fuel tanks. The craft is 15.24 m long and 3.7 m high at the rotor hub.

* How does FLIRS work?

Forward-looking infra-red (FLIRS) is a way of sensing infra-red rays – heat. Infra-red is similar to light rays but the waves are longer and carry heat energy. Like night vision goggles, FLIRS looks in front of a helicopter, plane, ship or vehicle to detect heat sources ahead. These might include the engines of other vehicles and craft, missiles, buildings, fires and even human bodies. FLIRS works by day or night and is not affected by rain or hazy conditions. The best systems can 'see' many kilometres in front, to help pilots and drivers steer the best course and avoid crashes.

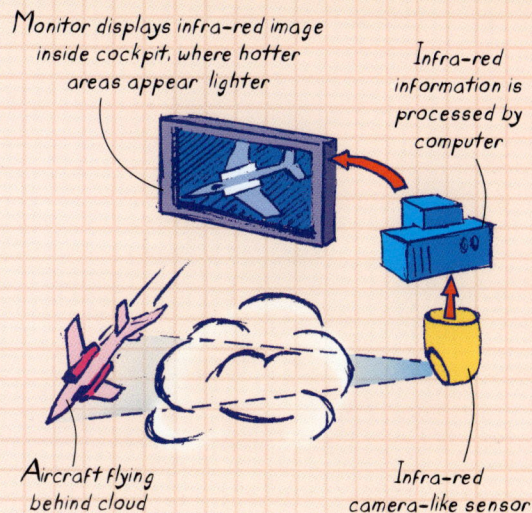

Monitor displays infra-red image inside cockpit, where hotter areas appear lighter

Infra-red information is processed by computer

Aircraft flying behind cloud

Infra-red camera-like sensor

Rotor hub

Main rotor The rotor design is termed semi-rigid, which gives good speed and agility. The rotor diameter is 12.8 metres.

Roof window

Flight deck and crew Pilot and co-pilot sit side by side at the front. The rear compartment has room for up to nine combat-ready troops, or a range of other people such as paramedics and wounded. Total payload is 750 kilograms.

In development is the Future Lynx, also called the Lynx Wildcat. It will not be quite as fast as the Lynx, but it will carry heavier loads and have a greater range.

The speed record-holding Lynx of 1986 had modified extra-powerful Gem engines and notched rotor blades.

Electronics Like most combat aircraft the Lynx has an array of radar and infra-red equipment in its nose section. Some Lynxes can tow sonar sounders to detect submarines in the water.

Torpedo

BELL X-1

As aircraft got faster and faster, their builders and pilots began to worry about the 'sound barrier'. They knew from general science that going above a certain speed causes a sonic boom (shock wave) – this is how lightning makes thunderclaps. Would an aircraft that went supersonic (faster than sound) shake to bits or even explode? On 14 October 1947 they found the answer was no, as the Bell X-1 broke the sound barrier.

X-1 test pilot 'Slick' Goodlin asked for a bonus of $150,000 to break the sound barrier. He was not chosen for the task.

Eureka!

The Bell X-1 was the first of the US X-plane programme. 'X' is for experimental and also for unknown or secret. The Xs are a mix of strange aircraft, missiles and rockets designed to test various kinds of new technology. Another famous X, the X-15, is on page 36.

Whatever next?

The newest aircraft designs are hypersonic, which is five times faster than the speed of sound, more than 5000 kilometres per hour (see page 36). Much above this, scientists are not sure what will happen.

Ethyl alcohol tank
The fuel or propellant was the substance ethyl alcohol – the same alcohol that is in beers, wines and spirits.

All-moving tailplane

6062

The Bell X-1 in front of its B-29 'mothership'

Rocket engine The Reaction Motors XLR11-RM3 rocket engine had four combustion chambers where fuel and oxidizer burned, producing almost 6000 pounds of thrust.

High-visibility paint

Sensor

✳ Into the UNKNOWN

Experts were unsure if the Bell X-1 could take off under its own power. Its wings were designed for enormous speed, and were too small to give enough lifting force at low speed. For the record attempt, the craft was carried into the air inside the altered bomb bay of a B-29 Superfortress (see page 26). The X-1 dropped and fell like a stone. Then pilot Chuck Yeager switched on the rocket engine to blast it higher and higher and go supersonic. Its rocket fuel finished, the plane glided down to land at Murdoc (now Edwards) Air Force Base. In 1949 Yeager managed to take off from an ordinary runway – the only time the X-1 did so.

Wings Unlike a normal aircraft wing, the X-1's wings were the same shape on the upper and lower surface, for 'laminar flow' – to generate no lift for a smooth, straight ride.

In 1953 Chuck Yeager went twice the speed of sound in a follow-up aircraft, the X-1A.

Watch a re-enactment of the record-breaking flight by *Bell X-1* by visiting www.factsforprojects.com and clicking on the web link.

The X-1 was designed as a 'bullet with wings', following the same shape as the bullets from the famous Browning .50 calibre machine gun.

Aneroid hollow discs or wafers contain air at ground pressure

Altimeter casing

Pointer

Altitude indication dial

Wafers expand as aircraft gains altitude due to lower outside air pressure

Gears, rods and levers transmit movement of wafers to the pointer

How do ALTIMETERS work?

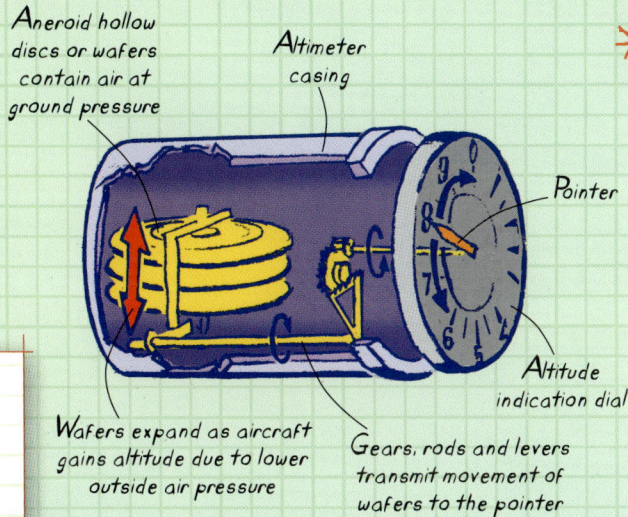

The altimeter is a device that measures altitude – how high it is. There is less air with height, giving less pressing force or air pressure. This lower air pressure allows a set of small chambers in the altimeter, which are filled with air at ordinary pressure, to get larger or expand. The expansion moves a series of levers and gears that register on a dial or display (see page 37). Heights are measured not from the ground, which goes up and down far too much, but from sea level.

LOX tank The X-1 needed no air intake for oxygen to burn its fuel. It carried its own supply as super-cooled liquid oxygen, LOX. This got around the problem of thin air with too little oxygen at great height.

The sound barrier was broken as the X-1 hurtled over the Mojave Desert of California, USA, at a height of 13,000 m.

Pilot Several test pilots flew the three X-1s. The record-breaking sound barrier flight was in the hands of US Air Force Captain Charles 'Chuck' Yeager. The tiny cockpit was smoothly contoured into the nose, with no bulge.

Data transmitter

Fuel pipe fairing

Explosive straps

Pitot to measure air pressure

GLAMOROUS GLENNIS

Bullet shaped fuselage The fuselage had almost no projections or side extensions, which would cause turbulence or swirling in the air flow at such high speed. The nitrogen spheres (right) provided pressure to push fuel into the rocket engine, rather than using a fuel pump.

Nitrogen gas spheres

The X-1 was small – just 9.45 m long and 3.3 m high, with wings 8.5 m across. Its take-off weight was about 6 tonnes – carried by a mothership (see page 30).

Glamorous Glennis For the sound barrier attempt the authorities allowed the X-1 to be named Glamorous Glennis after the wife of pilot Chuck Yeager.

The flow of air into the pitot (see page 37) showed that the Bell X-1 reached a top speed of 1127 km/h.

CONCORDE

The only supersonic passenger plane to go into full service was Concorde. There were 20 Concordes, built during the 1960s-70s by a partnership between Britain and France. The first test flight was from Toulouse in France in March 1969. Only two airlines, British Airways and Air France, bought them. The last official landings occurred in 2003 and most Concordes are now in museums.

Eureka!

The idea for SST, SuperSonic Transport, goes back to the early 1950s. While Concorde was being tested, the US started their own version, the Boeing 2707. But it was cancelled in 1971 due to cost and environmental worries.

Whatever next?

It's doubtful that there will be another superfast jetliner. Fuel costs, pollution and noise problems mean modern aircraft are slower but quieter and cleaner.

Concorde could cruise at an altitude of 18,000 m, which is twice as high as most passenger jetliners.

Concorde's cruising speed was about 2100 km/h. It had a top speed of 2330 km/h, which was 2.2 times faster than the speed of sound.

Visor After take-off, when the nose had been raised, a heat-resistant visor slid over the flight deck windows for extra safety and streamlining. At full speed the cockpit windows became too hot to touch.

Cabin doors Because of Concorde's crusing height, the specially designed doors had to cope with much greater pressure difference between inside and outside than on other passenger aircraft.

Radio antenna

Nose The nose cone was 'drooped' by 5 degrees for take-off, raised for level flight, then lowered again by 12.5 degrees for landing (see opposite).

BRITISH AIRWAYS

Narrow fuselage During the 1960s when Concorde was being developed, most airlines had a narrow body or fuselage. Wide-bodied jets arrived in the 1970s.

Concorde's fuselage was narrow compared to modern airliners

* Faster than a BULLET

People who travelled on Concorde rarely forgot the experience. But it was a small plane with a narrow body and only four seats in each row. It carried just 120 passengers (the latest Airbus A380 holds up to 800), with no modern features such as in-flight movies. The ride was also noisy and shaky compared to today's quiet jetliners. However there was luxury service with the best food and drink. But the tickets were amazingly expensive. Gradually people decided that they would rather pay much less and arrive at their destination a couple of hours later.

Concorde could fly from London or Paris to New York in just 3.5 hours. With the time difference across the Atlantic, this meant that going by local time, passengers arrived before they took off!

Take a virtual tour of Concorde's cabin by visiting www.factsforprojects.com and clicking on the web link.

Concorde's landing speed was about 300 km/h – almost three times the UK motorway speed limit.

Elevons The two-part elevons at the rear of the delta wings controlled going up or down, or pitch. Only the inner part was used at high speed.

Fin

At take-off, when fully loaded for a long flight, Concorde weighed almost 190 tonnes. About half of this weight was fuel.

Engines Concorde was powered by four Rolls Royce-SNECMA Olympus 593 afterburning turbojets, each weighing more than 3 tonnes. By today's standards they were extremely noisy.

Engine intake

Leading edge

Delta wing The delta shape is stronger than a normal wing design and cuts through the air better at great speed.

Windows The passenger windows were small. This was partly for strength, and also to reduce the rate of air pressure loss in the cabin in the event of one breaking.

Fuel tanks To keep the aircraft properly balanced, pumps moved the fuel between various tanks to shift the weight distribution as Concorde sped up and slowed down.

As Concorde heated up from the intense air friction at full speed, its overall length increased by about 30 cm.

In July 2000 a Concorde crashed in flames near Paris, France, killing 113 people. The airlines later decided to retire the jetliner. The last three British flights landed one after the other at Heathrow Airport, London in October 2003.

✳ How do DROOP-SNOOTS work?

Concorde had to have the best in streamlining, with a very long, sharp nose, and small flight deck windows to cope with the intense heat and pressure at full speed. But this meant that as the plane came down with its nose angled up, ready to land, the pilots could not see the runway. The answer was the 'droop-snoot'. The nose tilted down on the approach to landing, to allow the pilots a clear view.

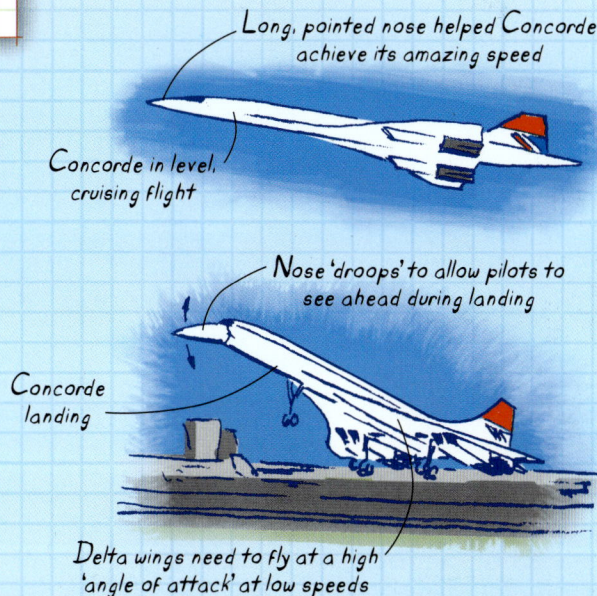

Long, pointed nose helped Concorde achieve its amazing speed

Concorde in level, cruising flight

Nose 'droops' to allow pilots to see ahead during landing

Concorde landing

Delta wings need to fly at a high 'angle of attack' at low speeds

SR-71 BLACKBIRD

Few shapes suggest sheer speed and power as much as the Lockheed SR-71A Blackbird. It was designed as a spy plane for the USA to keep an eye on Russia and nearby countries during the 'Cold War' of the 1960s–70s. At this time the two powerful nations, with their huge amounts of nuclear weapons, argued greatly. The Blackbird first flew in 1964. Its specialities were long-range, very high-flying reconnaissance (spying) – and breaking records.

Eureka!

The very first aircraft used in warfare, in the early 1900s, were spy planes. They droned slowly over the enemy army, so that observers could count troop numbers and positions. Soldiers below tried to shoot them down.

Whatever next?

It's possible that Blackbird's air speed record will never be broken. Instead of superfast planes, we now have all kinds of satellites to spy on each other. Or we use remote-controlled aircraft called drones, which are usually quite slow.

In total, 32 Blackbirds were built and 20 remain. The other 12 were lost in non-combat accidents.

Star-tracking The navigation systems included a star-tracker that could detect pinpoints of starlight even during daytime.

Crew The incredible speed and altitude meant that crew had to wear pressure suits to survive ejecting in an emergency (see opposite).

Paintwork The very dark blue colour reduced the chance of the aircraft being seen against a background of the night sky.

Blackbirds served the US military for 34 years up until 1998.

Radar

Pitot

Fuselage The titanium metal panels covering the fuselage only fitted loosely when the Blackbird was on the ground. At speed they heated up and expanded by several centimetres to give a tight fit.

Small chines were also fitted to the sides of the engine pods

Section through forward fuselage

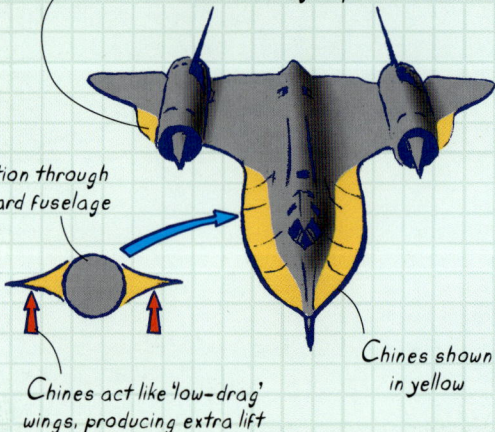

Chines act like 'low-drag' wings, producing extra lift

Chines shown in yellow

✳ How do CHINES work?

The Blackbird's main fuselage had sharp ridges along the sides at the front, which merged into the main wings behind. These ridges are called chines. Some of the plane's designers suggested the idea, but others were not impressed. So they built many wind tunnel models and found that chines were very helpful. They gave extra lift to keep the plane up, and they made it more steady at low speeds. Many modern fast aircraft have similar features, although smaller.

Like the fuselage, the fuel tanks of the Blackbird had tiny gaps when cool. So they leaked JP-7 jet fuel until the aircraft had heated to working temperature.

To see the incredible Blackbird in flight visit www.factsforprojects.com and click on the web link.

The Blackbird was 32.7 m long and had a wingspan of 16.94 m.

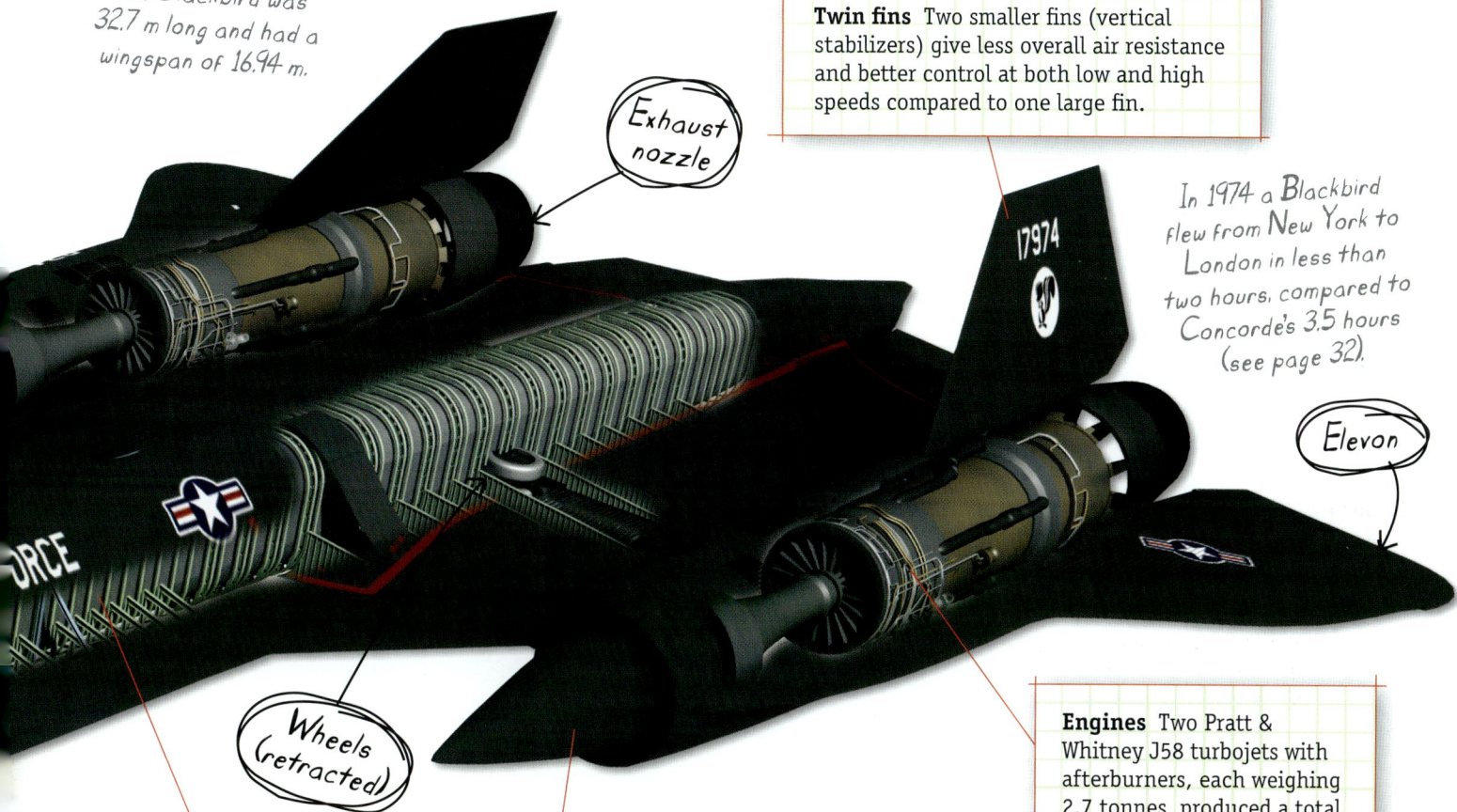

Exhaust nozzle

Twin fins Two smaller fins (vertical stabilizers) give less overall air resistance and better control at both low and high speeds compared to one large fin.

17974

In 1974 a Blackbird flew from New York to London in less than two hours, compared to Concorde's 3.5 hours (see page 32).

Elevon

Wheels (retracted)

Massive fuel tanks The Blackbird had a full-tank range of 5400 kilometres but it was often fuelled several times in mid air, after coming down a few thousand metres.

Spike The sharp, cone-shaped 'spike' at the engine air intake was positioned forwards for take-off and slow flight. Then it slid backwards by 66 centimetres to reduce shock waves at high speed.

Engines Two Pratt & Whitney J58 turbojets with afterburners, each weighing 2.7 tonnes, produced a total output of more than one million horsepower.

Loaded and ready to take off, the Blackbird weighed 78 tonnes – the same as an Airbus A320 180-seater short-medium airliner.

In 1976 the Blackbird set two world records. One was the fastest speed of any non-rocket manned aircraft, at 3530 km/h. The second was for aircraft height with an altitude of 25,929 m.

✳ Almost ASTRONAUTS

For low-level missions the Blackbird's cockpit could be pressurized and air-conditioned like a normal aircraft. So the two crew members wore standard jet fighter pilot helmets, oxygen masks and flying suits. For high-altitude missions they wore full pressure suits, similar to spacesuits. These supplied air and kept them cool – even with cockpit air conditioning, the inside of the windscreen got hotter than boiling water. Improved designs of the pressure suit became standard wear for space shuttle crew.

The crew of the Blackbird looked like they were heading into space

NORTH AMERICAN X-15

In 1967 US pilot Pete Knight took the record for the fastest speed of all aircraft, in the X-15 rocket plane. The X-15 already held the record for the highest flight of any aircraft, achieved in 1963 with pilot Joe Walker. As part of the X-plane's programme (see page 30), this amazing flying machine did almost everything except actually going into orbit.

Eureka!

The X-15 was designed to research how aircraft handle at higher altitudes where there is little or no air. It last flew in 1968.

Whatever next?

Rocket planes have now merged with spacecraft. In 2004 SpaceShipOne went up into space, more than 100 kilometres high, and landed safely.

Wedge section fin

XLR99 throttled rocket engine Most rocket engines gain full power within a few seconds of start and then stay fully on. The Reaction Motor XLR99 was throttled, meaning the pilot could adjust its thrust between half and full power. The engine's 'burn time' was between 80 and 150 seconds.

Anhydrous ammonia fuel The substance burnt by the on-board oxygen was greatly cooled and pressurized anhydrous ammonia, a form of the chemical ammonia (NH_3) that usually exists as a horrible-smelling, suffocating gas.

FUEL VENT
FUEL JETT

NASA
66671

USAF

Pete Knight's manned aircraft speed record is 7274 km/h, set in 1967.

Jettison-ready lower fin

The X-15 landed on rear skids – there was no room for rear wheels

✳ Rocket-powered SKID

Like the Bell X-1, the North American X-15 (built by the company North American Aviation) was not intended to take off under its own power. It could never carry enough fuel to go from ground level all the way to the edge of space. So it was carried aloft under the wing of a giant B-52 bomber. Before landing the lower part of the rear fin came away, or jettisoned, otherwise it would slice into the ground.

Only three X-15s were built, each slightly different from the others. They made 199 flights with 12 test pilots. One pilot was Neil Armstrong – the first person to walk on the Moon.

Watch an animation of the launch and flight of the X-15 by visiting www.factsforprojects and clicking on the web link.

In 1963, Joe Walker set an altitude record is 107.8 km in an X-15. He reached space briefly. Officially, space starts at a height of 100 km.

Diaphragm

ASI casing   ASI dial

Ram air is forced into the diaphragm, making it expand

Pitot tube

'Ram' air enters pitot tube

Pitot tube can be mounted on wing or nose of aircraft

Gears, rods and levers transmit movement of diaphragm to the pointer

Pointer

How does an ASI work?

To show their speed, fast machines need an ASI (air speed indicator). The simplest versions work by sensing the pressure of air in a small pipe, the pitot tube. If you run faster, the wind feels stronger on your face. The faster an aircraft goes, the more air tries to force its way into the pitot tube. It raises the air pressure inside and pushes on a flexible sheet, the diaphragm, which bends inwards. The bending moves a series of levers and gears linked to a dial. Air speed equipment is often combined with altitude-sensing devices to form a pitot-static system.

Wings Stubby wings gave the X-15 just enough stability and control to fly straight at top speed and then land safely.

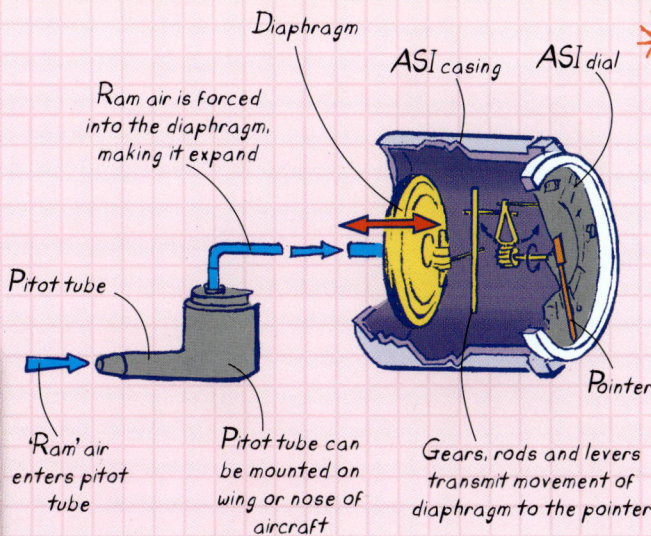

Sharp leading edge

LOX (liquid oxygen oxidizer) Like the Bell X-1 (see page 30), the North American X-15 had to take its own supply of oxygen in liquid form to burn its fuel. There is almost no air, and so no oxygen, at the edge of space. At full power the engine consumed more than 70 kilograms of fuel and oxidizer per second.

The X-15 was 15.45 m long and 4.12 m high. Its wingspan was only 6.8 m – less than half the length. The modified second aircraft, the X-15A-2, was 0.5 m longer.

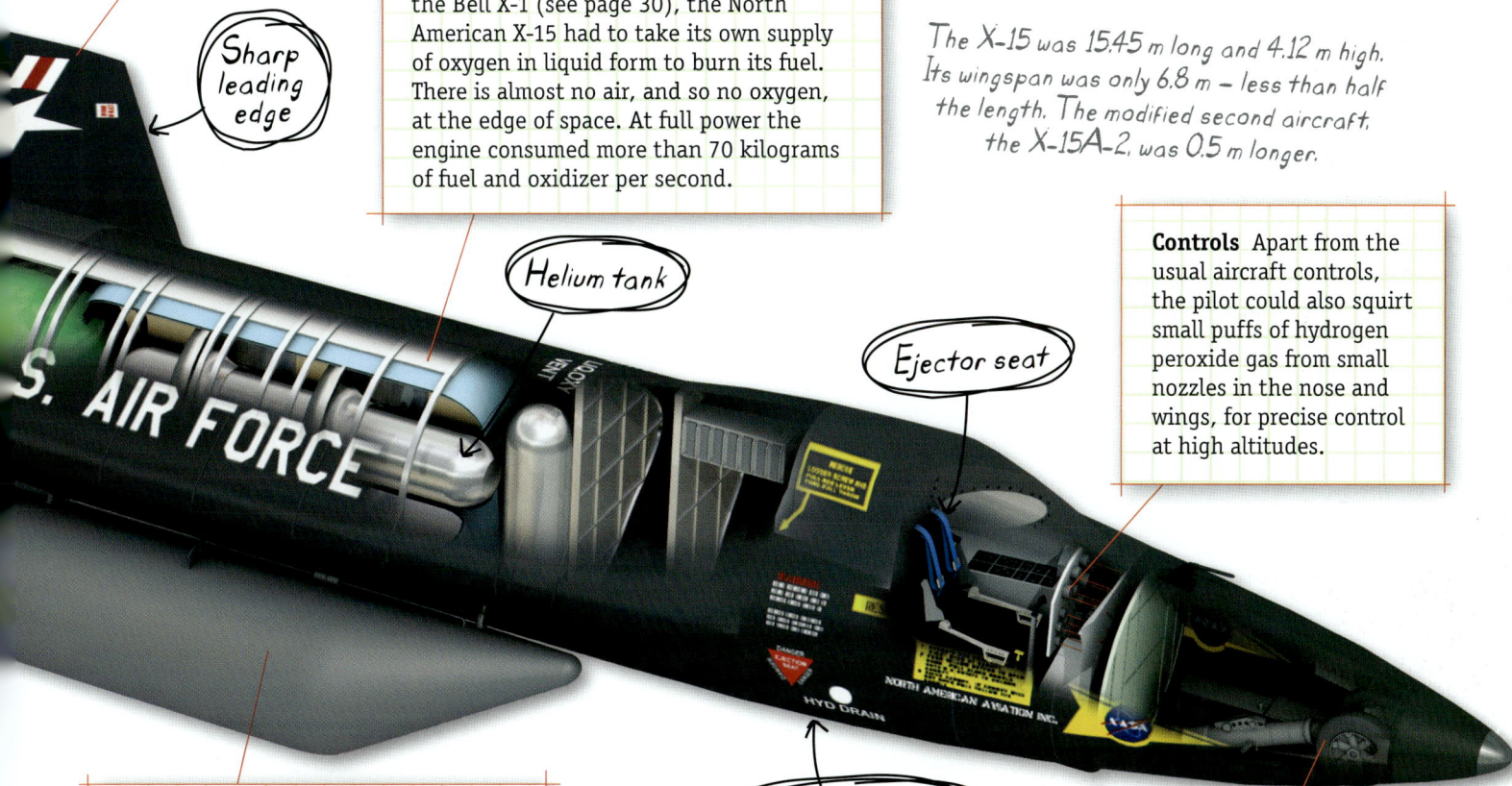

Controls Apart from the usual aircraft controls, the pilot could also squirt small puffs of hydrogen peroxide gas from small nozzles in the nose and wings, for precise control at high altitudes.

S. AIR FORCE

Helium tank

Ejector seat

Heat-proof paint

Drop-off fuel tanks The second-built craft, X-15-2, was damaged when landing. It was rebuilt slightly longer and with extra fuel tanks that could fall away, and renamed the X-15A-2. This was the plane that took the ultimate air speed record. But heat damage meant it had to be retired.

After mid-air launch and the rocket 'burn', the X-15's flight lasted about ten minutes. It ended with a landing at over 300 km/h.

Retracted nose wheel The nose wheel could not be steered. So the X-15 had to land on a long, wide dry lake bed rather than on an ordinary runway, which would be too narrow.

GLOSSARY

Alloy
A combination of metals, or metals and other substances, for special purposes such as great strength, extreme lightness, resistance to high temperatures, or all of these.

Antenna
Part of a communications system that sends out and/or receives radio signals, microwaves or similar waves and rays. Most antennae (also called aerials) are either long and thin like wires or whips, or dish-shaped like a bowl.

Blade
In aircraft, one of the long, slim parts of a propeller (airscrew) or helicopter rotors. Some propellers have six blades or more.

Bullet
Usually a short, rod-shaped, solid metal or plastic object with a pointed front end, fired out of a gun or similar weapon.

Calibre
In weapons, the inside width or diameter of a tube such as a gun barrel.

Chassis
The main structural framework or 'skeleton' of a vehicle, that gives it strength, and to which other parts are fixed, like the engine and seats.

Crankshaft
The main turning shaft in an engine, which is made to rotate by the up-and-down movements of the pistons.

Cylinder
In an engine or mechanical part, the chamber inside which a well-fitting piston moves.

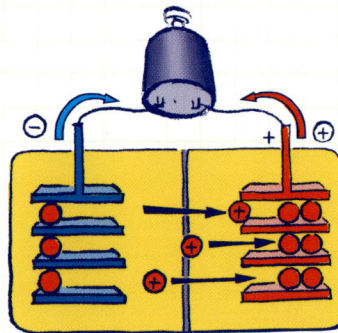

Li-ion cell

Damper
A part that reduces or dampens movements, usually sudden jolts or to-and-fro vibrations. On vehicle suspensions it is sometimes called the shock-absorber.

Diesel engine
An internal combustion engine (one that burns or combusts fuel inside a chamber, the cylinder), which uses diesel fuel, and causes this to explode by pressure alone rather than by a spark plug.

Disc brake
A braking system where two stationary pads or pistons press onto either side of a rotating flat disc attached to the wheel, to slow it down.

Drive shaft
A spinning shaft from an engine or motor that drives or powers another part, such as the propeller of a water vessel or the wheels of a car.

Elevator
The control surface of an aircraft, usually on the tailplane (small rear wing), that makes it tilt up or down (pitch).

Elevon
The control surface of a tail-less or 'flying wing' aircraft, which is a combined elevator and aileron.

Fin
The upright part at the rear of most aircraft, also known as the vertical stabilizer and often called the tail.

Friction
When two objects or substances rub or scrape together, causing wear and losing movement energy by turning it into sound and heat.

Fuel
A substance with lots of chemical energy in the form of its matter or substance. We usually release this energy for use by burning.

Fuselage
The main body or central part of an aircraft, usually long and tube-shaped.

Gears
Toothed wheels or sprockets that fit or mesh together so that one turns the other. If they are connected by a chain or belt with holes where the teeth fit, they are generally called sprockets.

Hull
The main body or central part of a water vessel like a ship, and also of some land vehicles such as tanks.

Hydraulic
Machinery or equipment that works using high-pressure liquid such as oil or water.

Altimeter

Infra-red

A form of energy, as rays or waves, which is similar to light but with longer waves that have a warming or heating effect.

Petrol engine

An internal combustion engine (one that burns or combusts fuel inside a chamber, the cylinder) that uses petrol fuel and causes this to explode using a spark plug.

Piston

A wide, rod-shaped part, similar in shape to a food or drinks can, that moves along or up and down inside a close-fitting chamber, the cylinder.

Pneumatic

Machinery or equipment that works by using high-pressure gas such as air or oxygen.

Propeller

A spinning device with angled blades, like a rotating fan, that turns to draw in a fluid such as water or air at the front, and thrust it powerfully rearwards.

Radar

Sending out radio waves that bounce or reflect off objects, and detecting the echoes to find out what is around.

Radiator

In cars and similar vehicles, a part designed to lose heat, for example, from an engine. It has a large surface area, usually lots of fins or vanes. Hot water from the engine circulates through it, to become cooler before flowing back to the engine.

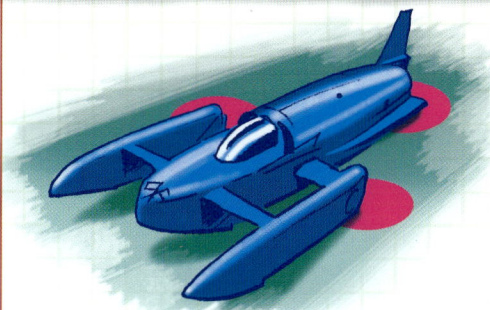

Bluebird K7

Radio

Signals and messages sent by invisible waves of combined electricity and magnetism, where each wave is quite long, from a few millimetres to many kilometres. (Light waves are similar but much shorter.)

Rudder

The control surface of an aircraft or watercraft, usually on the upright fin or 'tail' of an aircraft or below the rear hull of a boat, that makes it steer left or right (yaw).

Satellite

Any object that goes around or orbits another. For example, the Moon is a natural satellite of the Earth. The term is used especially for artificial or man-made orbiting objects, particularly those going around the Earth.

Sprocket

A wheel with teeth around the edge, often called a gear wheel. Unlike gears, sprockets do not fit together or mesh directly, but have a chain or belt or similar between them.

Suspension

Parts that allow the road wheels or tracks of a vehicle to move up and down separately from the driver and passengers, to smooth out bumps and dips in the road. Also any similar system that gives a softer, more comfortable ride.

Tailplane

The two small rear wings on most aircraft and some helicopters, also known as the horizontal stabilizers. They carry the elevators and are usually next to the fin or 'tail'.

Throttle

A control that allows more fuel and air into the engine for greater speed, sometimes called an accelerator.

Transmission

In land vehicles, all the parts that transmit the turning force from the engine (crankshaft) to the wheel axles, including the gears, gearbox and propeller shaft.

Turbojet

A jet engine with fan-like turbine blades inside, which produces a powerful blast of gases from the rear end.

Turboshaft

A jet engine with fan-like turbine blades inside, which spins a shaft for power rather than using a blast of gases.

Wingspan

The distance of an aircraft's main wings from one tip or end to the other.

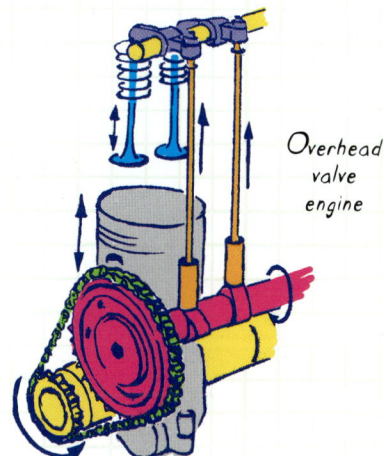

Overhead valve engine

INDEX